HOW TO MARKET
TO CONSUMERS

10 Ways To Win

JOHN A. QUELCH

Harvard Business School

WILEY

John Wiley & Sons

NEW YORK · CHICHESTER · BRISBANE · TORONTO · SINGAPORE

Copyright © 1989 by John A. Quelch
Published by John Wiley & Sons, Inc.

Library of Congress Cataloging in Publication Data:

Quelch, John A.
  How to market to consumers.

  Bibliography: p.
  1. Marketing—United States. 2. Advertising—
United States. I. Title.

HF5415.1.Q45 1988   658.8   88-17331
ISBN 0-471-61853-5

Printed in the United States of America

10 9 8 7 6 5 4 3 2 1

Preface

Marketing managers in consumer goods and services companies today face an environment of increasing complexity. Trends such as consumer segmentation, media fragmentation, trade concentration, industry deregulation, global competition and an explosion in market information are presenting formidable challenges to consumer marketers that will continue into the 1990s. This book does not profess to cover all the challenges that the consumer marketer will face in the next decade. My hope, however, is that the reader, whether a practicing manager or interested student, will find that many of the most topical issues in consumer marketing are addressed in a readable yet analytically rigorous fashion and that the frameworks and recommendations presented will contribute to better decision making.

During the past decade, I must have talked to hundreds of marketing and sales managers in consumer goods and services firms about their problems and challenges. Their insights and opinions have been invaluable as I have developed the analytical frameworks and prescriptive recommendations presented in the papers reproduced in this book.

Of equal significance are the many colleagues at Harvard Business School and elsewhere with whom I have been fortunate enough to work. In particular, I would like to acknowledge Paul W. Farris and James M. Olver of the University of Virginia, Kristina Cannon-Bonventre of Northeastern University, Hirotaka Takeuchi now at Hitotsubashi University in Tokyo, Japan, Edward J. Hoff, a Harvard University Ph.D. candidate, and Frederic Alper, President of Morris Alper & Sons, a prominent New England food brokerage.

I am also grateful to *Business Horizons*, *Harvard Business Review*, *Journal of Consumer Marketing* and *Sloan Management Review* for permitting me to include in this book articles published initially in these journals. My thanks also to their reviewers and editors for helping my colleagues and me improve upon the quality of the manuscripts that we initially submitted.

Much of the material in the book represents the output of research projects funded by the Division of Research at the Harvard University Graduate School of Business Administration. No other business school in the world does more to encourage its faculty to interact with, learn from, and contribute to practicing managers. Were I not associated with such an institution, this book would not have been possible.

Finally, I would like to thank John Mahaney at Wiley for his encouragement and advice in shepherding this book to publication.

JOHN A. QUELCH

Lincoln, Massachusetts
October 1988

Contents

Contents

Chapter Three
Global Marketing
53

Chapter Four
Local Marketing
77

Chapter Five
Dual Marketing
93

Chapter Six
Licensing
115

Chapter Seven
Nonstore Marketing
127

Chapter Eight
Point-of-Sale Marketing
149

Chapter Nine
Promotion and Advertising
165

Contents

HOW TO MARKET
TO CONSUMERS

Introduction

Consumer Marketing in the 1990s

M arketing managers in consumer goods and services companies today face a much more complex and challenging environment than their predecessors. Some of these environmental changes are outside the control of the individual marketer. During the past decade, for example, the marketing manager has alternatively had to operate in a high inflation, recessionary economy and in a low inflation, expansionary economy. Many industries from telecommunications to the airlines that were tightly regulated a decade ago are now subject to market forces as a result of deregulation. The antitrust laws, once vigorously enforced, are these days given short shrift in the face of acquisitions and mergers designed to build larger companies that are better able to compete for market share in an increasingly global marketplace. Beyond these changes in the economic and regulatory environment, we can identify six additional areas where environmental change is causing consumer marketers to reevaluate their approaches to the development and implementation of marketing strategies and programs but where the marketer's ability to influence and respond to change is greater. As we enter the 1990s, it is more imperative than ever that marketing managers stay alert to their environment and develop an ability to fashion marketing strategies and organizations to changing environmental circumstances.

CONSUMER SEGMENTATION

During the 1960s consumer goods firms set about mass marketing a stream of new products through the mass media. By the end of the 1980s, it was clear that the mass market no longer existed, at least in its pure form. Recent census data indicated the increasing demographic heterogeneity of American society. For example, only 8% of households comprised the traditional nuclear family of husband, nonworking spouse and two children. As overall U.S. disposable income increased, groups such as seniors, teens, blacks, and Hispanics, that had hitherto received only modest attention from advertisers, were increasingly targeted with specific products and advertising. A further factor contributing to the demise of the mass market was the search for individuality of expression on the part of the Baby Boom generation that, by the late 1980s, represented one-third of the U.S. population but two-thirds of its spending power. For the Baby Boomer, the fact that a product or brand was used by more consumers than any other was often regarded as a negative and was unlikely to be emphasized in advertising.

While demographic heterogeneity continues to prompt the development of marketing programs targeted more precisely at particular segments, marketers pursuing demographic segmentation continue to face two problems. First, there is considerable heterogeneity within each seemingly homogeneous demographic group. The Hispanic segment, for example, comprises consumers from many different cultural backgrounds. Second, research indicates that a proportion of each demographic minority group wishes to be treated as part of the mainstream population and does not necessarily welcome being singled out for special marketing attention.

Increased demographic heterogeneity is not only fueling the interest of consumer marketers in segmentation, but also causing them to examine more closely segmentation approaches beyond demographics. We see these days, partly as a result of economic prosperity, increased attention to lifestyle and psychographic segmentation. This trend is evident in:

- The frequent introductions of premium products from imported beers to platinum credit cards, the advertising for which invariably emphasizes lifestyle benefits as much as, if not more than, functional benefits.

- The rapid growth of specialty retailing concepts such as Ralph Lauren and Banana Republic that aim to sell consumers on a lifestyle concept and persuade them to become totally outfitted in coordinated apparel, thereby increasing the consumer's average dollar purchase level.

- The growing popularity among marketers of research services such as Stanford Research Institute's VALS Service that enables marketers to identify zip codes and census tracts populated predominantly by households with lifestyles similar to those of their target consumers.

Notwithstanding the growing interest in lifestyle segmentation, it remains unclear whether the majority of consumers adapt their lifestyles as they progress through their life cycles or alternatively seek to retain their early lifestyles and associated brand loyalties as they age.

The decline of the mass market is evident in geographic as well as demographic terms. The book, *The Nine Nations of North America*,[1] highlighted the cultural and economic diversity among regions of the United States in the 1980s as some prospered while others languished. In response, most consumer marketers are paying more attention to regional marketing. In other words, they are customizing the marketing program from one region to another in response to different consumer preferences, distribution channel structures, and/or competitive pressures. Paradoxically, as they target more narrowly defined, geographical segments in the domestic marketplace, consumer marketers in multinational companies are also interested in identifying homogeneous segments of consumers across countries that they can target with the same marketing program worldwide.

The demise of the mass market and the shift toward more rigorous market segmentation presents a number of challenges to consumer marketers. First, marketers have to be able to gather, analyze, and act on additional information about the size, growth trend, and means of accessing individual market segments. A more acute understanding of the benefit preferences and decision-making processes of each segment is required and extra care in media planning is necessary if different messages are to be targeted at different segments.

Hence, consumer marketers must spend more time on market research and on developing their skills in segmentation and positioning. Marketers of high-share, mainstream brands find themselves increasingly facing competition from niche products targeted at segments of the mass market. They frequently respond by introducing additional varieties under the same or similar brand names in order to serve an increasingly segmented marketplace. However, if cannibalization and confusion are to be minimized, it is essential that these line extensions be positioned clearly to consumers and the trade.

For the niche marketer, on the other hand, the challenge is to identify a product positioning that is clearly communicable to the target segment despite the increasing clutter of new product introductions, that is not faddish but sustainable in the marketplace at a profitable margin, and that is defensible against competition. Only if these criteria are met can the extra costs associated with developing a customized product and program for a niche segment be justified.

MEDIA PROLIFERATION

The growing interest in segmentation is both resulting from and contributing to a proliferation of alternative media vehicles targeted at ever finer market segments. New specialist magazines focusing on particular sports, activities, and interests are launched every week. Partly in response, the major national magazines such as *Newsweek* and *Time* are now published in multiple editions with advertising and editorial content tailored by geographic region and by reader profile in order to boost both sales and advertising effectiveness. In the electronic media, the share of the prime time television audience commanded by the three national networks continues to decrease as increased household penetration of cable television and satellite television bring multiple new viewing options into many homes. The need for programming for cable television channels has resulted in programs being developed for much narrower audiences than the mass market orientation of broadcast television could ever justify.

The proliferation of media options is just one ingredient in the broader and more complex marketing communications mix that today's consumer marketer faces. Expenditures on alternative communications approaches such as public relations, point-of-sale merchandising, and direct marketing continue to outpace expenditures on media advertising.

A well-orchestrated public relations program incorporating corporate image advertising can provide a very cost effective means of communicating a name and message to a broad target audience for any product or service that is newsworthy, that is of interest to a wide number of consumers, and that perhaps lends itself to demonstration in visual media. For example, Reebok International has spent no more than $25 million a year on media advertising for its brand of athletic footwear and apparel during each of the past three years yet commands a tremendous brand name recognition among consumers, partly as a result of a sophisticated public relations program that involves sponsorships of sports events at national, regional, and local levels. Moreover, the development of special event promotions has become especially important for tobacco and liquor manufacturers whose ability to reach their consumers through traditional advertising media has been severely restricted by legislation. One caveat is in order: marketers must carefully manage public relations efforts to avoid raising consumer expectations unjustifiably, for example in the pharmaceutical industry, when it appears that a new ''wonder drug'' has been discovered.

The successful launch of L'eggs pantyhose in the early 1970s involved the use of an innovative package, display fixture, and point-of-sale product identification chart. This and similar success stories prompted manufacturers to pay more attention to ensuring that their point-of-sale materials were attention getting and effective. Expenditures on point-of-sale displays and signs continue to expand faster than advertising expenditures due to their comparative cost effectiveness and to the increasing percentage of consumer brand and product purchase decisions that are not preplanned but made on impulse at the point-of-sale. At the same time, consumer insistence on longer store opening hours means that stores increasingly have to rely on part-time salespeople, many of whom are uneducated about the features of the products they are selling. As a result, manufacturers are having to depend on point-of-sale display fixtures and merchandising materials to attract and educate their potential customers and influence their decision-making processes.

A third growth area in the marketing communications mix is direct marketing that caters to time-pressured dual-income households with more money to spend, less time to spend it, and a strong desire for shopping convenience. Under the direct marketing umbrella, we include approaches ranging from simple direct mail catalogs to telemarketing using toll-free numbers to the Home Shopping Network to teleshopping using interactive videotex. The direct marketing approaches with the broadest appeal are those, as we might expect, that require the least adaptation from traditional shopping behavior. Thus, direct mail catalogs have proliferated, while interactive videotex has failed to fulfill its early promise and is still very much a technology in search of a market. One advantage of direct marketing is that it enables manufacturers to circumvent increasingly powerful channel intermediaries and communicate directly with consumers without investing in retail real estate. Through direct marketing, the marketer can also build a data base of his/her consumers that can be used for market research.

The broadening of the marketing communications mix means that media selection and scheduling are more complex than ever before. We need to understand better how to measure the relative impacts of different forms of marketing communication in order to ensure the optimal allocation of marketing resources among the alternatives. The increasing importance of the media buying function in advertising agencies and the growing interest in media stewardship (involving a continuing audit of a company's media options and plans) are further testimony to the growing complexity of the media decisions facing consumer goods and services marketers.

INFORMATION EXPLOSION

Consumer marketers today are having to contend with much more market information than existed a decade ago, information that is typically more timely, more complete, and more accurate. The advent of low cost data processing and of desk top computing that enable any manager to access on-line data bases has been both a response and a stimulus to the further proliferation of market research information. In addition, more sophisticated market research techniques have become cost-justifiable as a result of lower data processing costs. Marketers are, therefore increasingly exploring how to use the information available as a source of competitive advantage to identify untapped market niches for new products, to explore trade-offs among various pricing, advertising, and promotion strategies and tactics, and to improve the efficiency with which marketing expenditures are allocated. Larger companies should be in a better position to invest the resources required to exploit the opportunities presented by the explosion of market research information.

As Porter[2] has noted, the power of information as a source of competitive leverage depends on its importance in adding value in the value chain and, second, on the degree to which product complexity or rapid technology change causes the customer to need more information.

In many companies, the information system has traditionally been run by a data processing group primarily for the benefit of the accounting department. This approach is being superceded by integrated decision-support systems providing analytical as well as data retrieval capabilities to all functions. The power of such systems can only be realized if the data bases on which they are based are integrated for use by all functions in the organization. For example, Fisher Camuto Corp. computers analyze retail sales data from the company's shoe stores around the United States on a daily basis and compute the number of pairs of different styles and sizes that the company's production plants in Brazil should manufacture the following day. This kind of system minimizes inventory carrying costs and, at the same time, ensures the prompt feedback of sales information from the marketplace into the production planning process.

There are several pitfalls that consumer marketers must avoid in the new information intensive environment. First, there is a risk that managers may become so preoccupied with analyzing every decision on their personal computers that additional information, far from speeding up and improving decision making, leads to "analysis paralysis." Second, there is the concern that managers may attempt to conduct statistically sophisticated analyses that are beyond their interpretative capabilities and to make faulty decisions as a result. A third concern is that an information-intensive marketing environment is likely to attract a different type of manager, perhaps someone who is less creative and more analytical, who would prefer to analyze market research data on the computer rather than interact directly with consumers and customers in the field, and who is likely to follow a more routinized, perhaps more tactical, approach to marketing decision making. If these and other problems associated with the implementation of marketing decision-support systems are to be avoided, managers will have to be properly trained, their expectations will have to be managed, the role of the marketing research department will have to be redefined, and systems will have to be implemented on a gradual basis.

TRADE POWER

There are five bases for competition in retailing: price, assortment, convenience, service, and ambiance. The past decade has seen the emergence of many new types or formats of retail stores, offering different mixes of these five benefits in order to cater to an increasingly segmented consumer population. In grocery retailing a decade ago, for example, a fairly standard supermarket catered to the mass market. By the late 1980s, consumers could choose from among multiple grocery retailing formats, including box stores offering a limited assortment of high turnover items at rock bottom prices to supercenters and hypermarkets offering very broad and deep assortments of both groceries and general merchandise and appealing to the one-stop shopper.

Many larger retailers have invested in multiple store formats to appeal to several consumer segments and to reduce risk through diversification. The largest, with capital to invest, are trying to accelerate consumer interest in new store formats in order to capture share from smaller competitors that lack similar resources to invest in store conversions or new construction.

Partly as a result, concentration in retailing is increasing, not so much on a national level as on an individual market level, meaning that an increasing percentage of retail sales in a particular city comes to be controlled by two or three chains. This trend toward market concentration, combined with correspondingly more sophisticated retail managements, is enhancing the power of the trade versus the manufacturer. Scanner information collected at the point-of-sale further enhances trade power by enabling retailers to identify quickly product turnover rates. In many cases, the trade buyer who once relied on the manufacturer salesperson for detailed information about a product category now has much more timely and detailed brand movement information than the salesperson, further tilting the power balance in the trade's favor. A final factor contributing to increased trade power is the growing percentage of consumer purchases that are made on impulse and therefore more subject to the influence of in-store advertising.

Increasing trade power means that store names are becoming as strong as, if not stronger than, manufacturer brand names. As a result, chains such as Neiman Marcus now offer considerable quantities of private label merchandise for which they contract directly with manufacturers. Quality differentials between private label and national brand merchandise are now often nonexistent or, at least, much less than the price premiums of the national brands attempt to imply. In some cases, the private label merchandise may be superior. A second motivation to add private label merchandise is that consumers are less able than they are in the case of national brands to comparison shop prices on the same item at several competing chains in the same trading area. Using its procurement skills, Loblaw's supermarkets in Canada has launched the President's Choice line of private label products that are *superior* to the national brands in addition to its traditional private label and generic product lines; the national brands are increasingly likely to be caught in a pincer between lower-priced and super-premium private labels.

What are the consequences of this shift in power from the manufacturer to the trade? First, there is a clear shift of marketing expenditures from advertising to sales promotion and merchandising support. While some of these additional promotion dollars merely represent adjustments to artificially inflated manufacturer prices, the trend also reflects an important shift in marketing philosophy from long-term franchise building through pull marketing to short-term, pay-as-you-go, push tactics. Many commentators believe that this can only detract from the long-term health of brand franchises. In other words, in order to respond to the growing power of the trade, manufacturers are shifting their marketing expenditures in a direction that is at one and the same time responsive but also conducive to furthering the trend.

A second consequence is the need for manufacturers to adapt their national marketing programs by class of trade, by geographic region, and according to the needs of individual key trade accounts. This may mean, for example, developing a merchandising, promotion, and product program that is specifically tailored to a particular account, perhaps including the manufacture of special "derivative" models which carry the manufacturer's brand name but are uniquely featured for a particular trade customer.

Increasingly, manufacturers will have to view their trade customers as partners rather than as adversaries. Often, this will require a change of mindset. In practical terms, it will result in much more contractual preplanning of quantities to be purchased at designated prices, of merchandising support, of delivery schedules, and other customer services. The largest manufacturers will be able to command a competitive edge over their smaller rivals through a more precise knowledge of their production and logistics costs and by providing more value-added services such as training for retail clerks and assistance to trade buyers in implementing forward buying and direct product profit systems.

PRODUCT INNOVATION AND QUALITY

The best defense against increasing trade power is the unique, differentiated product that offers important benefits to consumers. However, while statistics compiled by Product Initiatives Group and others indicate that the rate of new consumer product introductions is greater today than ever before, the average level of innovativeness associated with these new products appears to be falling. Most new product introductions are merely line extensions that do not incorporate any innovation—whether in product design, packaging, or distribution system—that offers markedly superior satisfaction to consumers.

There are five principal reasons for this focus on line extensions:

- Most producers are seeking to use excess manufacturing capacity, and line extensions can be manufactured with little additional capital investment on the same production lines as the core product. On the other hand, a proliferation of line extensions adds to demand forecast error and production scheduling complexity, the costs of which are rarely charged to marketing management.

- The interest in market segmentation has prompted a proliferation of "flavor-of-the-month" line extensions designed to cater to every conceivable taste.

- Because the technologies on which consumer goods are based are mature, the gap between private label and national brand quality is closing. In the face of ever-improving private label products and aggressive competition from other national brands, manufacturers are desperate to retain their shelf space at the point-of-sale; line extensions are often viewed as a way of achieving this objective.

- The cost efficiencies associated with umbrella branding as opposed to the economic risk associated with launching new brand names have fueled interest in line extensions under a single brand umbrella. The problem with this trend is that, in the new product development process, a new concept that might offer the promise of being launched as a new product under its own brand name will all too often be designated as a potential line extension, with correspondingly diminished potential for adding incremental sales and profits.

- The short-term pressure on senior executives for increased quarterly earnings per share to defend their companies against takeover or acquisition attempts is reflected in a correspondingly short-term perspective toward product policy. This manifests itself in frequent launches of line extensions at the expense of allocating resources to the development of breakthrough product concepts that may be more risky and take longer to develop, yet be more innovative and of more enduring value to the company.

In the face of these incentives toward mediocrity, marketers with the resources to do so must redouble their research and development efforts to ensure a constant stream of innovative, differentiated products that can sustain price premiums in the marketplace without the need for frequent price promotion. Stockholders in many consumer goods and services firms should be prepared in the 1990s to accept dividend cuts if necessary to ensure that such R&D investment can be sustained.

Marketers should also recognize that marketing innovation need not necessarily come from the laboratory. For example, L'eggs pantyhose was not merely a product innovation but also a packaging, advertising, and distribution system innovation.

At the same time as innovation is emphasized, it must not be at the expense of product quality. Marketers during the 1990s will need to pay more attention to understanding how different segments of consumers define quality. The component dimensions of quality must be uncovered and marketers must focus on delivering superior quality on those "jugular" dimensions that consumers use to choose among brand alternatives. These dimensions of quality may relate not merely to the physical product but also to the range of services that are provided along with the product both prior to, during, and after the purchase. Consumer goods marketers have much to learn from industrial- and service-marketers services on how to provide quality service after the sale has been made. I have always been impressed by the following statement from the founder of Matsushita Industrial Electric Company who states: "The responsibility of a manufacturer cannot be relieved until its product is disposed of by the end consumer."[3] American managers would probably limit the time frame of their responsibility to the period until the warranty expired. Setting high standards of responsibility as Matsushita does inevitably translates into a much greater attention to product and service quality. Only if such high standards are set will they stand a chance of being achieved and will American manufacturers be able to improve their competitiveness in the global marketplace.

THE MARKETING FUNCTION

The consumer marketer of the 1990s will need to stay closer to the consumer than ever before. Given the pace of change in the consumer marketplace and the continuing emergence of new consumer segments, every marketing manager should allocate a day or two each month to talk with consumers, trade customers, and salespeople in the field. Given the time pressure that the marketing manager will be under in the increasingly complex environment we have described, it will be tempting to shortchange these essential field visits. No marketing manager should consider himself or herself too senior to undertake such field trips. At Procter & Gamble and other companies, the most senior executives have assigned themselves key trade accounts and go into the field to meet with the top executives of these accounts once every quarter.

But if only marketing managers stay close to the consumer, this will be insufficient. It is essential that a customer orientation be developed throughout all functions of the organization.* In the past, marketing and sales managers have been overly protective of their role as the exclusive points of contact with consumers and trade customers respectively. This approach, while facilitating coordinated communication, may cause more problems than it solves because other functions in the organization, lacking the customer perspective, find it much harder to understand the demands that marketing managers often make to meet customer needs. Marketing's working relationships with the other functions can be eased if all managers had an equal understanding of and interest in the consumer. Many Japanese companies, for example, encourage their engineers to visit with consumers in the field and to commission their own market research. In the customer-oriented firm of the future, the market research department is increasingly likely to be a corporate staff group rather than a function controlled by and available only to marketing management. In short, knowledge of the consumer is too important to be left solely in the hands of marketing management.

In many firms, marketing has traditionally been the lead function with profit and loss responsibility and, as a result, has had a tendency to treat the other functions as staff support groups. In the future, however, marketing management will have to view the other functions in the organization more as partners. For two reasons, the marketing function's star has fallen somewhat in the past decade. First, the end of double-digit inflation revealed many marketing inefficiencies that the price in-

---

*Note that we use the term "customer orientation" rather than "marketing orientation." The latter term may imply an effort by the marketing function to extend its influence.

creases justified by the inflation of the 1970s had concealed. Second, an annual rate of population growth in the United States of less than 1% has meant that primary demand in many product categories can no longer be readily expanded. The resulting market share struggle in many product categories has prompted firms to look to manufacturing and procurement efficiencies in addition to market expansion to improve their bottom line profit margins. The role and importance of other functions in what had hitherto been marketing-driven organizations has therefore increased.

The continuance of this trend will mean that successful marketing vice presidents of the 1990s will be more likely than their predecessors to have had multifunctional experience including a tour of duty in another department. Second, they will be more likely to have had an international assignment reflecting the increasing globalization of markets. Third, they will be individuals who lead through team building rather than fiat because there will be increasing use of multifunctional project and venture teams to shepherd new products from the concept stage to commercialization as fast as possible.

Given the changing environment that marketing managers face, there will be increasing experimentation with new marketing organization structures. The traditional product management system has proved very resilient since it began at Procter & Gamble in the 1920s, partly because the task mix of the product manager can be adapted easily to the needs of any product-market situation. However, the system is now showing signs of strain. The increasing importance of push versus pull marketing, of sales promotion versus advertising, of regional and trade marketing versus the national marketing program, all support an increased role for the field sales force which interacts directly with trade customers. We are likely to see the overlay in product management organizations of trade marketing and account management functions that replicate those used by industrial marketers such as IBM.

The structure of the marketing organization itself will, in the interests of productivity, be increasingly tailored to the career development requirements of its managers and to the actual and potential importance of individual brands. Some brands may be sufficient in actual and potential sales to warrant dual brand managers, one dealing with strategic issues and one dealing with tactical and execution-sensitive tasks, while other brands may be too small to warrant the attention of even one brand manager and may therefore be assigned to an associate brand manager. The marketing organization chart of the future is less likely to be a study in symmetry but, as a result, may well be more efficient.

A key challenge facing the marketing manager of the 1990s will be how to measure the productivity of the marketing function to justify corporate resource allocations. Given the considerable pressure on most consumer marketers to control costs and overheads, adding additional marketing personnel, whether line or staff managers, is no longer as easy as it once was. The quest for a leaner marketing organization at a time when increasing environmental complexity is putting managers under extreme time pressure requires that individuals of the highest quality be attracted to the marketing function. These individuals will have the ability to develop and articulate a clear vision for their businesses, to see the forest from the trees, and to focus their efforts on activities that will do most to leverage the performance of their businesses. At the same time, they will be versatile managers who are street-smart implementers as well as strategic thinkers. Companies will have to pay top dollar for individuals of this calibre, but should not shrink from doing so.

Many of the new ideas in marketing organization will come not from the mainstream packaged-goods companies that will seek to adapt their product management systems to the new environment rather than to abandon them but, rather, from the rapidly growing consumer services sector. From restaurants to mutual funds, consumer service organizations interact directly with their consumers so it is essential that operations personnel have a customer orientation. The marketing function is often a headquarters staff support group organized on a market management system, with each manager responsible for defining the needs of a key market segment and developing the bundle of services and products needed to meet them. In an increasingly segmented environment, organizing around market managers as opposed to product managers is likely to become more common.

CONCLUSION

We have reviewed six environmental trends that will continue to challenge the consumer marketer through the 1990s: consumer segmentation; media proliferation; the explosion in market information; trade power; the need for product innovation and quality; and the role of the marketing function. We have tried to emphasize how these trends are closely interlinked.

It is important to note how closely these trends are interlinked, and to emphasize that the responses developed by tomorrow's marketing managers must likewise be integrated rather than piecemeal and mesh into a cohesive corporate strategy.

One

——

Quality Marketing

Corporate executives and consumers have in recent years adopted divergent views of product quality. Several recent surveys indicate how wide the quality perception gap is:

- Three out of five chief executives of the country's largest 1,300 companies said in a 1981 survey that quality is improving; only 13% said it is declining.[1] Yet 49% of 7,000 consumers surveyed in a separate 1981 study said that the quality of U.S. products had declined in the past five years. In addition, 59% expected quality to stay down or decline further in the upcoming five years.[2]

- Half the executives of major American appliance manufacturers said in a 1981 survey that the reliability of their products had improved in recent years. Only 21% of U.S. consumers expressed that belief.[3]

- Executives of U.S. auto manufacturers cite internal records that show quality to be improving each year. "Ford quality improved by 27% in our 1981 models over 1980 models,'' said a Ford executive.[4] But surveys show that consumers perceive the quality of U.S. cars to be declining in comparison with imported cars, particularly those from Japan.

Mindful of this gap, many U.S. companies have turned to promotional tactics to improve their quality image. Such efforts are evident in two trends. The first is the greater emphasis advertisements place on the word *quality* and on such themes as reliability, durability, and workmanship. Ford, for instance, advertises that "quality is job one," and Levi Strauss proffers the notion that "quality never goes out of style." And many ads now claim that products are "the best" or "better than" competitors'.

The second trend is the move to quality assurance and extended service programs. Chrysler offers a five-year, 50,000 mile warranty; Whirlpool Corporation promises that parts for all models will be available for 15 years; Hewlett-Packard gives customers a 99% uptime service guarantee on its computers; and Mercedes-Benz makes technicians available for roadside assistance after normal dealer service hours.

While these attempts to change customer perceptions are a step in the right direction, a company's or a product's quality image obviously cannot be improved overnight. It takes time to cultivate customer confidence, and promotional tactics alone will not do the job. In fact, they can backfire if the claims and promises do not hold up and customers perceive them as gimmicks.

To ensure delivery of advertising claims, companies must build quality into their products or services. From a production perspective, this means a companywide commitment to eliminate errors at every stage of the product development process—product design, process design, and manufacturing. It also means working closely with suppliers to eliminate defects from all incoming parts.

Equally important yet often overlooked are the marketing aspects of quality-improvement programs. Companies must be sure they are offering the benefits customers seek. Quality should be primarily customer-driven, not technology-driven, production-driven, or competitor-driven.

In developing product quality programs, companies often fail to take into account two basic sets of questions. First, how do customers define quality, and why are they suddenly demanding higher quality than in the past? Second, how important is high quality in customer service, and how can it be ensured after the sale?

As mundane as these questions may sound, the answers provide essential information on how to build an effective customer-driven quality program. We should not forget that customers, after all, serve as the ultimate judge of quality in the marketplace.

THE PRODUCTION-SERVICE CONNECTION

Product performance and customer service are closely linked in any quality program; the greater the attention to product quality in production, the fewer the demands on the customer service operation to correct subsequent problems. Office equipment manufacturers, for example, are designing products to have fewer manual and more automatic controls. Not only are the products easier to operate and less susceptible to misuse but they also require little maintenance and have internal troubleshooting systems to aid in problem identification. The up-front investment in quality minimizes the need for customer service.

Besides its usual functions, customer service can act as an early warning system to detect product quality problems. Customer surveys measuring product performance can also help spot quality control or design difficulties. And of course detecting defects early spares later embarrassment and headaches.

Quality-Improvement Successes

It is relevant at this point to consider two companies that have developed successful customer-driven quality programs: L.L. Bean, Inc. and Caterpillar Tractor Company. Although these two companies are in different businesses—L.L. Bean sells outdoor apparel and equipment primarily through mail order while Caterpillar manufactures earthmoving equipment, diesel engines, and materials-handling devices, which it sells through dealers—both enjoy an enviable reputation for high quality.

Some 96.7% of 3,000 customers L.L. Bean recently surveyed said that quality is the attribute they like most about the company. Bean executes a customer-driven quality program by:

- Conducting regular customer satisfaction surveys and sample group interviews to track customer and noncustomer perceptions of the quality of its own and its competitors' products and services.

- Tracking on its computer all customer inquiries and complaints and updating the file daily.

- Guaranteeing all its products to be 100% satisfactory and providing a full cash refund, if requested, on any returns.

- Asking customers to fill out a short, coded questionnaire and explain their reasons for returning the merchandise.

- Performing extensive field tests on any new outdoor equipment before listing it in the company's catalogs.

- Even stocking extra buttons for most of the apparel items carried years ago, just in case a customer needs one.

Despite recent financial setbacks, Caterpillar continues to be fully committed to sticking with its quality program, which includes:

- Conducting two customer satisfaction surveys following each purchase, one after 300 hours of product use and the second after 500 hours of use.

- Maintaining a centrally managed list of product problems as identified by customers from around the world.

- Analyzing warranty and service reports submitted by dealers, as part of a product improvement program.

- Asking dealers to conduct a quality audit as soon as the products are received and to attribute defects to either assembly errors or shipping damages.

- Guaranteeing 48-hour delivery of any part to any customer in the world.

- Encouraging dealers to establish side businesses in rebuilding parts to reduce costs and increase the speed of repairs.

HOW DO CUSTOMERS DEFINE QUALITY?

To understand how customers perceive quality, both L.L. Bean and Caterpillar collect much information directly from them. Even with such information, though, pinpointing what consumers *really* want is no simple task. For one thing, consumers cannot always articulate their quality requirements. They often speak in generalities, complaining, for instance, that they bought "a lemon" or that manufacturers "don't make 'em like they used to."

Consumers' priorities and perceptions also change over time. Taking automobiles as an example, market data compiled by SRI International suggest that consumer priorities shifted from styling in 1970 to fuel economy in 1975 and then to quality of design and performance in 1980.[5] (See Table 1.1.)

In addition, consumers perceive a product's quality relative to competing products. As John F. Welch, chairman and chief executive of General Electric Company, observed, "The customer . . . rates us better or worse than somebody else. It's not very scientific, but it's disastrous if you score low."[6]

One of the major problems facing U.S. automobile manufacturers is the public perception that imported cars, particularly those from Japan, are of higher quality. When a 1981 *New York Times*–CBS News poll asked consumers if they thought that Japanese-made cars are usually better quality than those made here, about the same, or not as good, 34%

Table 1.1. CHANGES IN THE IMPORTANCE TO CUSTOMERS
OF U.S. AUTOMOBILE CHARACTERISTICS

	1970	1975	1980
1	Styling	Fuel economy	Quality
2	Value for money	Styling	How well-made
3	Ease of handling and driving	Prior experience with the make	Fuel economy
4	Fuel economy	Size and weight	Value for money
5	Riding comfort	Ease of handling and driving	Riding comfort

answered better, 30% said the same, 22% said not as good, and 14% did
not know. When the Roper Organization asked the same question in
1977, only 18% said better, 30% said the same, 32% said not as good,
and 20% did not know.[7]

Further, consumers are demanding high quality at low prices. When
a national panel of shoppers was asked where it would like to see food
manufacturers invest more, the highest-rated response was "better quality
for the same price."[8] In search of such value, some consumers are even
chartering buses to Cohoes Manufacturing Company, an apparel specialty
store located in Cohoes, New York that has a reputation for offering
high-quality, designer-label merchandise at discount prices.

Consumers' perceptions of product quality are influenced by various
factors at each stage of the buying process. Some of the major influences
are listed in Table 1.2.

Table 1.2. FACTORS INFLUENCING CONSUMER PERCEPTION OF QUALITY*

BEFORE PURCHASE	*AT POINT OF PURCHASE*	*AFTER PURCHASE*
Company's brand name and image	Performance specifications	Ease of installation and use
Previous experience	Comments of salespeople	Handling of repairs, claims, warranty
Opinions of friends	Warranty provisions	Spare parts availability
Store reputation	Service and repair policies	Service effectiveness
Published test results	Support programs	Reliability
Advertised price for performance	Quoted price for performance	Comparative performance

*Not necessarily in order of importance.

Watching for Key Trends

What should companies do to improve their understanding of customers' perspectives on quality? We know of no other way than to collect and analyze internal data and to monitor publicly available information.

Internally generated information is obtained principally through customer surveys, interviews of potential customers (such as focus group interviews), reports from salespeople, and field experiments. Recall how L.L. Bean and Caterpillar use these approaches to obtain data on how their current and potential customers rate their products' quality versus those of competitors'.

Publicly available information of a more general nature can be obtained through pollsters, independent research organizations, government agencies, and the news media. Such sources are often helpful in identifying shifts in societal attitudes.

Companies that try to define their customers' attitudes on product and service quality often focus too narrowly on the meaning of quality for their products and services; an understanding of changing attitudes in the broader marketplace can be equally valuable.

Toward the end of the last decade, too many U.S. companies failed to observe that the optimism of the mid-1970s was increasingly giving way to a mood of pessimism and restraint because of deteriorating economic conditions. Several polls taken during the 1970s indicated the nature and extent of this shift[9]; for instance, Gallup polls showed that while only 21% of Americans in the early 1970s believed "next year will be worse than this year," 55% held this pessimistic outlook by the end of the 1970s.

Pessimistic about what the future held, consumers began adjusting their lifestyles. The unrestrained desire during the mid-1970s to buy and own more gave way to more restrained behavior, such as "integrity" buying, "investment" buying, and "life-cycle" buying.

Integrity purchases are those made for their perceived importance to society rather than solely for personal status. Buying a small, energy-efficient automobile, for example, can be sign of personal integrity. Investment buying is geared toward long-lasting products, even if that means paying a little more. The emphasis is on such values as durability, reliability, craftsmanship, and longevity. In the apparel business, for example, more manufacturers have begun stressing the investment value of clothing. And life-cycle buying entails comparing the cost of buying with the cost of owning. For example, some might see a $10 light bulb, which uses one-third as much electricity and lasts four times as long as a $1 conventional light bulb, as the better deal.

These changes in buying behavior reflect the pessimistic outlook of consumers and their growing emphasis on quality rather than quantity: "If we're going to buy less, let it be better."

By overlooking this fundamental shift in consumer attitudes, companies missed the opportunity to capitalize on it. If they had monitored the information available, managers could have identified and responded to the trends earlier.

ENSURING QUALITY AFTER THE SALE

As we suggested earlier, the quality of customer service after the sale is often as important as the quality of the product itself. Of course, excellent customer service can rarely compensate for a weak product. But poor customer service can quickly negate all the advantages associated with delivering a product of superior quality.

At companies like L.L. Bean and Caterpillar, customer service is not an afterthought but an integral part of the product offering and is subject to the same quality standards as the production process. These companies realize that a top-notch customer service operation can be an effective means of accomplishing the following three objectives:

(1) *Differentiating a company from competitors.* As more customers seek to extend the lives of their durable goods, the perceived quality of customer service becomes an increasingly important factor in the purchase decision. Whirlpool Corporation promises to stand by its products rather than hide behind its distribution channels; it has parlayed a reputation for effective customer service into a distinct competitive advantage that reinforces its image of quality.

(2) *Generating new sales leads and discouraging switches to alternative suppliers.* Keeping in regular contact with customers so as to deliver new information to them and gather suggestions for product improvements can ensure the continued satisfaction of existing customers and improve the chances of meeting the needs of potential purchasers.

(3) *Reinforcing dealer loyalty.* Companies with strong customer service programs can also broaden their distribution channels

more easily to include outlets that may not be able to deliver high levels of postpurchase customer service on their own.

The Customer Service Audit

To be effective, a customer service operation requires a marketing plan. Customer services should be viewed as a product line that must be packaged, priced, communicated, and delivered to customers. An evaluation of a company's current customer service operation—a customer service audit—is essential to the development of such a plan.

A customer service audit asks managers the following questions:

- *What are your customer service objectives?* Many companies have not established objectives for their customer service operations and have no concept of the role customer service should play in their business and marketing strategies. Every company should know what percentage of its revenue stream it expects to derive from service sales and whether the goal is to make a profit, break even, or—for reasons of competitive advantage—sustain a loss.

- *What services do you provide?* It is useful to develop a grid showing which services your company provides or could provide for each of the products in your line. These might include customer education, financing arrangements, order confirmation and tracing, predelivery preparation, spare-parts inventory, repair service, and claims and complaints handling.

- *How do you compare with the competition?* A similar grid can be used to chart the customer services your competitors provide. Through customer surveys, you can identify those areas of customer service in which your company rates higher or lower than the competition. In areas where your company is weak, can you invest to improve your performance? Where you are strong, how easy is it for competitors to match or exceed your performance?

- *What services do your customers want?* There is little value in developing superior performance in areas of customer service most customers consider only marginally important. An essential ingredient of the audit is, therefore, to understand the relative importance of various customer services to current and potential customers. Distinct customer segments can often be identified according to the priorities they attach to particular services.

- *What are your customers' service demand patterns?* The level and nature of customer service needed often change over the product's life. Services that are top priority at the time of sale may be less important five years later. Companies must understand the patterns and timing of demand for customer services on each of their products. These they can graph, as Figure 1.1 shows.

Product A in the figure is a security control system, an electronics product with few moving parts. A high level of service is needed im-

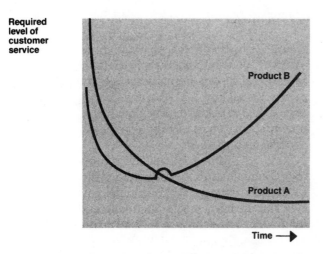

Figure 1.1. Postpurchase Service Demands for Two Products.

mediately following installation to train operators and debug the system. Thereafter, the need for service quickly drops to only periodic replacement of mechanical parts, such as frequently used door switches.

Product B is an automobile. Service requirements are significant during the warranty period because of customer sensitivity to any aesthetic and functional defects and also because repairs are free (to the customer). After the warranty period, however, service requirements beyond basic maintenance will be more extensive for B than for A, since there are more mechanical parts to wear out.

- *What trade-offs are your customers prepared to make?* Excellent service can always be extended—at a price. You should know the costs to your company of providing assorted customer services through various delivery systems (an 800 telephone number, a customer service agent, a salesperson) at different levels of performance efficiency. At the same time, you should establish what value your customers place on varying levels of customer service, what level of service quality they are prepared to pay for, and whether they prefer to pay for services separately or as part of the product purchase price.

Customers are likely to differ widely in price sensitivity. A printing press manufacturer, for example, has found that daily newspaper publishers, because of the time sensitivity of their product, are willing to pay a high price for immediate repair service, whereas book publishers, being less time pressured, can afford to be more price conscious.

THE CUSTOMER SERVICE PROGRAM

The success of the marketing program will depend as much on effective implementation as on sound analysis and research. After reviewing several customer service operations in a variety of industries, we believe that managers should concentrate on the following seven guidelines for effective program implementation:

(1) *Educate your customers.* Customers must be taught both how to use and how not to use a product. And through appropriate training programs, companies can reduce the chances of calls for highly trained service personnel to solve simple problems. General Electric recently established a network of product education centers that purchasers of GE appliances can call toll-free. Many consumer problems during the warranty period can be handled at a cost of $5 per call rather than the $30 to $50 cost for a service technician to visit a consumer's home.

(2) *Educate your employees.* In many organizations, employees view the customer with a problem as an annoyance rather than as a source of information. A marketing program is often needed to change such negative attitudes and to convince employees not only that customers are the ultimate judge of quality but also that their criticisms should be respected and acted on immediately. The internal marketing program should incorporate detailed procedures to guide customer-employee interactions.

(3) *Be efficient first, nice second.* Given the choice, most customers would rather have efficient resolution of their problem than a smiling face. The two of course are not mutually exclusive, but no company should hesitate to centralize its customer service operation in the interests of efficiency. Federal Express, for example, recently centralized its customer service function to improve quality control of customer-employee interactions, to more easily monitor customer service performance, and to enable field personnel to concentrate on operations and selling. The fear that channeling all calls through three national centers would depersonalize service and annoy customers used to dealing with a field office sales representative proved unwarranted.

(4) *Standardize service response systems.* A standard response mechanism is essential for handling inquiries and complaints. L.L. Bean has a standard form that customer service personnel use to cover all telephone inquiries and complaints. As noted earlier, the documented information is immediately fed into a computer and updated daily to expedite follow-through. In addition, most companies should establish a response system to handle customer problems in which technically sophisticated people are called in on problems not solved within specific time periods by lower-level employees.

(5) *Develop a pricing policy.* Quality customer service does not necessarily mean free service. Many customers even prefer to pay for service beyond a minimum level. This is why long warranty periods often have limited appeal; customers recognize that product prices must rise to cover extra warranty costs, which may principally benefit those customers who misuse the product.[10] More important to success than free service is the development of pricing policies and multiple-option service contracts that customers view as equitable and easy to understand.

Because a separate market exists for postsale service in many product categories, running the customer service operation as a profit center is increasingly common. But the philosophy of "selling the product cheap and making money on the service" is likely to be self-defeating over the long term, since it implicitly encourages poor product quality.

(6) *Involve subcontractors, if necessary.* To ensure quality, most companies prefer to have all customer services performed by in-house personnel. When effectiveness is compromised as a result, however, the company must consider subcontracting selected service functions to other members of the distribution channel or to other manufacturers. Otherwise the quality of customer service will decline as an aftermath of cost-cutting or attempts to artificially stimulate demand for customer service to use slack capacity. Docutel, the automated teller manufacturer, for example, transferred responsibility for customer service operations to Texas Instruments because servicing its small base of equipment dispersed nationwide was unprofitable.

(7) *Evaluate customer service.* Whether the customer service operation is treated as a cost center or a profit center, quantitative performance standards should be set for each element of the service package. Do an analysis of variances between actual and standard performances. American Airlines and other companies use such variances to calculate bonuses to service personnel. In addition, many companies regularly solicit customers' opinions about service operations and personnel.

CONCLUSION

In conclusion, we must stress that responsibility for quality cannot rest exclusively with the production department. Marketers must also be active in contributing to perceptions of quality. Marketers have been too passive in managing quality. Successful businesses of today will use marketing techniques to plan, design, and implement quality strategies that stretch beyond the factory floor.

Two

Premium Marketing

In this day when everything from mustard to diapers to cheese is readily available in an upscale version, what explains the growing trend to marketing the premium product? What are the characteristics of product categories susceptible to premium marketing? How can mainstream marketers respond to the threat—or opportunity—of expanding premium segments in the markets they serve? What strategic risks and growth challenges face the traditional established premium marketer? And how can a company become a successful premium marketer?

THE GROWTH OF PREMIUM MARKETING

In many product-markets, a premium segment is either emerging or growing in size and importance. Many factors are contributing to this trend.

As the rate of population growth in the United States has slowed, many mainstream marketers have become more interested in creating,

PROFILING THE PREMIUM PRODUCT

Although the characteristics of what is meant by "premium" vary by category, premium brands are typically of excellent quality, high priced, selectively distributed through the highest quality channels, and advertised parsimoniously.

Excellent quality is a sine qua non, and it is important that the premium marketer maintains and develops leadership in quality. This leadership will usually be based on technical superiority in those product categories where functional attributes and price-performance comparisons drive consumer decision making.

In categories where psychic benefits dominate decision making, the cultivation of a prestige image will often be the basis of leadership. Image leadership is derived partly from the relative exclusivity that a premium price and distribution channel give to the item, but it can be reinforced by a well-selected brand name, logo, and packaging, and by communicating the product's heritage, place of origin, or the personality behind it. All of these factors were attended to in the marketing of Perrier as "nature's soft drink."

When a premium product commands both technical and image leadership—for example, a Rolls Royce automobile—it typically enjoys both a significant comparative advantage and a defensible niche.

The premium segment can exist in almost any product category. Consumers willing to pay higher prices for premium products typically view them as one or more of the following:

- Affordable indulgences (Haagen Dazs ice cream);
- Tasteful gifts (Coach handbags);
- Smart investments (Maytag laundry appliances); or
- Status symbols (Mercedes Benz cars).

Some product categories, however, seem to be more susceptible to premium marketing than others. Although coffee and beer are both beverages, premium marketing strategies have been more successful to date for beer than for coffee. Why?

In the first place, coffee is a mundane, everyday item, more of a commodity. Beer is more of an indulgence. As such, it is more open to appeals to the taste of the self-styled connoisseur.

In a social situation, moreover, the brand of beer a consumer chooses is clearly visible. The choice is a social statement. Coffee, by contrast, is usually served anonymously from a pot.

Furthermore, the consumer is heavily involved in preparing a cup of coffee. Right down to adding too much or too little cream and sugar, it is quite possible for the consumer to make a bad cup from good-quality instant or ground coffee. On the other hand, beer is consumed straight from the bottle; the manufacturer's quality reaches the consumer intact.

When, however, coffee is served in social situations, there is higher risk; therefore, a consumer is more likely to use a premium brand. The percentage of market sales likely to be accounted for by premium brands of coffee is less than that for beer.

In assessing the evolution of the premium segment in any product category, it is well to bear in mind several important points.

- *The meaning of "premium" may vary from one market segment to another.* Older Americans regard Cadillac as a premium automobile; younger Americans are more likely to mention Mercedes or BMW. Increasingly, we find traditional premium products being challenged by nouveau premium products, often higher priced and destined either to supplant their aging rivals or·to be mere fads. Will Calvin Klein's Obsession fragrance, though lacking demonstrable technical superiority and any historical heritage, supplant Chanel No. 5 as the premier perfume? Or will it fade into oblivion after a couple of seasons?

- *The meaning of "premium" may change over time* as consumer lifestyles and technologies evolve. Often, the mainstream marketer interested in obtaining a slice of the premium segment will attempt to change the criteria for what is regarded as premium. By making electronic features an important benefit to consumers purchasing major appliances, General Electric displaced KitchenAid as the premium brand of dishwashers. Conversely, the premium marketers with the greatest longevity are often found in categories characterized by little change in technologies and consumer needs—for example, jewelry and silver flatware.

- *The premium segment may be perceived as delivering different levels of "premiumness."* In product-markets where the premium segment grows in size, a distinction is frequently drawn between premium and *super*premium products. This phenomenon is evident, for example, in the beer market, where Heineken might now be considered merely a premium brand while Samuel Adams might be characterized as *super*premium.

- Sometimes, *the premium product will not, by one standard of judgment, be technically superior.* Hand-blown glassware, for example, is more likely to have irregularities than machine-made glassware. These irregularities do not, however, detract from the product's functionality; paradoxically, the flaws are visual indicators that the glassware is hand-crafted and, therefore, more expensive.

MAINSTREAM MARKETERS MOVING UP

What strategic options are open to the mainstream marketer facing the challenge of increasing consumer interest in premium entries? There are five options which are not necessarily mutually exclusive:

(1) Introduce a premium version of the existing mainstream brand;

(2) Introduce or acquire a brand with a name unconnected to that of the existing mainstream brand;

(3) Trade up a loyal base of consumers from a mainstream franchise when these satisfied customers make repeat purchases;

(4) Change the consumer's definition of ''premium'' to weaken the franchise of existing premium brands; or

(5) Redouble marketing efforts for the mainstream brand.

Introduce a Premium Version of a Mainstream Brand

Introducing a premium version of a mainstream brand is typically cheaper and faster than launching a new brand. Shell SU2000 gasoline, Ramada Renaissance hotels, and Maxwell House Master Blend coffee are three examples of this approach.

Because the new entry capitalizes on the already developed consumer recognition for the mainstream brand, it is not difficult to obtain consumer and trade interest. In addition, a premium entry can, if so promoted, cast a halo of quality across the entire brand franchise. However, despite these advantages, problems may arise.

- Stretching the existing brand name can dilute the clarity of its positioning in an increasingly segmented market.

- Advertising justification for the higher price of the premium entry may detract from the quality of the mainstream entries in a product line. General Electric faced this problem when it introduced its PermaTuf tub liner (with a ten-year warranty) only on its higher priced dishwashers.

- The premium version of a mainstream brand cannot compete convincingly with premium brands that have no poor relations in the mainstream. While the Corvette may help sell other Chevrolets, the image of those other products limits the Corvette's ability to compete convincingly against Porsche.

- Trade channels may not distinguish between the premium version and the mainstream brand. General Foods' attempt to position Maxwell House Master Blend as a premium item was thwarted when the trade aggressively price-promoted the premium product just as it did regular Maxwell House.

- If a manufacturer is selling different quality products through distribution channels of varying quality, all under the same brand franchise, there is a constant temptation to let the premium entry be sold through the lower quality distribution channels.

- If growth of the premium segment proves to be short-lived, the strength of the mainstream franchise will have been unreasonably jeopardized.

- The interests of the premium entry are often subordinated to those of the mainstream brand. The premium entry is not considered important enough to receive special management or sales force attention and is therefore presented to the trade and, ultimately, to the consumer in the same fashion as a mainstream brand. Even though the sales growth rate of the premium product may be superior, the dominant consideration is to protect current sales of the mainstream brands.

Introduce or Acquire a New Brand

The second option, to introduce or acquire a new brand, represents more commitment to the premium segment. It often involves a separate organization independent of the mainstream franchise. This option is especially appropriate when the perceptual gap between the mainstream brand and the premium segment is too great for the first option to stand a chance. A new premium brand can be internally developed or obtained through acquisition or a licensing arrangement. Some examples:

- Holiday Inns has developed a new chain, Embassy Suites, to tackle the premium end of the hotel market.

- Huffy, the bicycle manufacturer, established a joint venture with Raleigh, the U.K. bicycle producer, to secure a piece of the premium segment of the market rather than trying to upgrade consumer perceptions of its existing franchise.

- The Shulton division of American Cyanamid, marketer of Old Spice, the leading medium-priced line of men's toiletries, licensed the right to use the Pierre Cardin name on an upscale line of fragrances. Licensing an established designer brand requires less investment than developing a new premium brand from scratch, but the licensee has little control over how the designer's image will evolve.

- After its experience with Maxwell House Master Blend, General Foods is tackling the premium coffee market with not one but several new brands. Masters Collection is targeted at consumers who equate coffee quality with raw beans, while the Gevalia line of Swedish coffees, distributed by direct mail, appeals to those who see quality embodied in a foreign heritage.

The multiple-brand approach is more appropriate than the first option for increasingly segmented markets. Although more costly up front, the mainstream franchise is not put at risk.

In addition, a company has more strategic flexibility. Marketing resources can be allocated among several brands serving different segments as evolving market circumstances dictate.

Finally, participation in multiple segments permits the marketer to exert some control over the relative growth of each. Anheuser-Busch, for example, originally positioned Michelob as a special-occasion beer for weekend use, simultaneously conveying a premium image while influencing the size of the premium segment.

Trade Up Loyal Customer Base

A third option is to penetrate the premium segment of a market by offering premium products under a mainstream brand to an existing base of loyal and satisfied consumers who have purchased mainstream products and are looking to trade up.

Using this approach, Japanese manufacturers of motorcycles and other consumer products have demonstrated that a mainstream brand franchise can be extended into the premium segment in the case of more functional, technical products. Harley-Davidson and the other traditional motorcycle manufacturers had retreated to the high-priced end of the market, expecting to be able to defend it. Indeed, they erroneously regarded the premium segment as a separate market. However, they discovered that, although the size of the premium segment expanded with consumers trading up from smaller motorcycles, many of these consumers wanted the same features (such as electronic ignition rather than kick-starting) that they had become used to on their smaller Japanese bikes. In this case, features and performance proved more important than an exclusive brand name in determining who controlled the premium segment.

Change Consumer's Definition of "Premium"

A fourth option is to try to upgrade the image of a mainstream brand. Marketers can give an upgrade program its best chance of success by trying to change the criteria that consumers use to determine the degree of "premiumness" offered by different brands in the market.

General Electric's leadership in applying electronics technology to dishwashers, which existing premium manufacturers such as KitchenAid did not have the resources to imitate rapidly, has enabled G.E. to upgrade its image from that of a middle-of-the-road manufacturer. Electronic controls rather than a hefty stainless steel tub are now the signature of the premium dishwasher. Because brand images, like prices, are harder to raise than lower, G.E.'s success is especially impressive.

However, such upward stretching of a brand name may well be easier in the case of products that are purchased primarily for functional rather than psychic benefits. It is also worth noting that G.E.'s control of the Hotpoint brand gave it additional strategic flexibility in upgrading the G.E. franchise; Hotpoint dishwashers could further penetrate the low-price end of the market as the G.E. image improved.

Concentrate on Mainstream Brand

A fifth option open to the mainstream marketer is to do nothing to endorse the legitimacy of the premium segment. The marketer can encourage the trade to dismiss the premium segment as faddish, small, and unlikely to grow, and it can emphasize the quality and value of its mainstream brands. Given the evolution of most markets toward price-quality segmentation and the strategic benefits of multisegment representation, this strategy seems risky.

Mainstream manufacturers are being pressured by competition from above and below. Scripto, for example, lost market share both to a low-cost producer, Bic, and to manufacturers of premium-quality pens such as Cross. Although the middle portion of the market to which Scripto continued to cling was not destroyed, it was seriously eroded in size as the market segmented.

PREMIUM MARKETERS UNDER PRESSURE

While mainstream marketers are at risk if they do not respond to premium brand competition, the premium market has its pitfalls. In product categories driven by functional benefits, the premium marketer is typically vulnerable to attack from below. In categories driven by psychic benefits, the principal risk is attack from above. The two most common failings of the premium marketer are being too conservative and too aggressive.

Too Conservative

Many premium marketers are family-owned businesses with a historical commitment to quality. It may be easier for them to be dedicated to quality through durability than it is for the publicly held company, which is often accused of perpetrating built-in obsolescence in the interests of sales. Not being under shareholder pressure for growth, these family businesses may prefer to continue their low profile. Their view is that expansion would attract attention and competition. Even though healthy competition would expand the total size of the premium segment, such companies often would sooner remain isolated in the small triangle at the top of the market pyramid.

Such an approach is fine so long as a niche is defensible. When it is not, mainstream marketers attempting to penetrate and grow the premium segment may raise the level of marketing expenditures in the segment and so put the traditional premium marketer under pressure. Here are three examples:

- Distillers, a well-known U.K. manufacturer of premium-quality whiskey and other alcoholic beverages, was recently under take-over pressure from Argyll, a marketer of lower-priced brands. One of Argyll's principal arguments to shareholders was that Distillers, by being too conservative, permitted the market share of premium brands such as Black and White and Johnnie Walker to erode while the premium segment as a whole was being expanded by new competition.

- By permitting G.E. to change the definition of "premium" in the dishwasher category to emphasize electronics, KitchenAid lost its command of the premium segment. Being a premium niche player, KitchenAid, like Harley-Davidson, lacked sufficient resources to invest in the new technology. It is now being acquired by Whirlpool, a mainstream brand, which regards KitchenAid as a vehicle for entry into the premium segment.

- Stride Rite has long been the premium quality manufacturer of shoes and sneakers for infants and young children. However, increasingly, younger children want to behave and dress like their older siblings or like adults, with the result that the premium marketers that serve these age groups, facing heavy competition in their own segments, are pressing against and eroding Stride Rite's niche. Unable to extend the Stride Rite franchise to older age groups, the company has responded by acquiring premium-quality shoe manufacturers serving these other market segments.

Too Aggressive

The adage "familiarity breeds contempt" is often the nemesis of the marketer of a premium brand. Many of the premium products of yesterday—Bulova watches, Izod shirts, Smirnoff vodka—are the standard products of today and lack a clear position in their respective markets.

Pressure on the premium marketer frequently comes from distribution channels wanting to upgrade their store images by carrying premium brands. Pressure for sales growth prompts the development of products and services at lower price points to broaden the appeal of the franchise. Such an approach is often justified on the grounds that it will attract into the brand franchise customers who can afford the low-priced item. The idea is that these consumers will trade up later to more expensive products.

In practice, however, such franchise expansion implies a loss of exclusivity that opens the door for a new competitive superpremium brand. Even when sales growth is accompanied by an improvement in quality, the very fact that more people have access to the brand detracts from its "premiumness."

This chain of events is especially likely to afflict premium products in categories where psychic and status benefits are prominent in the purchase decision-making process. For example, Cadillac hurt its reputation and failed to attract younger buyers with its compact Cimarron, a thinly disguised but much more expensive Chevrolet Cavalier. The numbers of Mercedes now on U.S. roads, combined with the introduction of the lower-priced 190 series, are thought to have helped Jaguar establish itself as a strong premium brand on the basis of greater exclusivity. A recent Jaguar advertisement states: "From a heritage of coachbuilders to kings and the sporting aristocracy of Europe comes the most exclusive Jaguar sedan you can own."

Other markets are even more vulnerable to superpremium entries. The premium hotel, for example, depends heavily on the quality of the fixed plant. This plant naturally deteriorates over time. A hotel's location, which is unchangeable, may also lose its appeal. These facts threaten any hotel chain's ability to maintain a premium position, independent of the growth rate of the chain. Thus, over the years, Sheraton has successively been supplanted as the premium hotel chain by Hilton, Hyatt, and Intercontinental.

Coping Strategies

What strategies can a premium marketer follow that will permit growth but, at the same time, minimize degradation of the brand franchise?

MULTIPLE LINES. Hartmann Luggage offers four lines of different quality at different price points. For this strategy to succeed, the differences between the lines must be clearly visible, and the logic of the price-quality relationships must be comprehensible to both consumer and the trade. Hartmann has been able to maintain its premium position while expanding the size of the segment. At the same time it has created a barrier to entry by making multiple lines the price of admission to that segment.

SEQUENTIAL FEATURING. Major fashion houses frequently distinguish between their premium-priced collections, displayed at the New York and Paris fashion shows and sold to a limited number of wealthy clients, and their classification merchandise: lower priced, with a broader appeal, and incorporating the features of last year's collections. In this industry, the profits derived from classification sales subsidize the development of collections, which cast a premium halo over the classification merchandise, for which, in turn, a premium price can be charged.

SELECTIVE BROADENING. The status associated with using a premium brand often depends upon its being recognized by those not having access to it. Almost anyone in the United States can afford a Polo T-shirt. Rather than detracting from the premium quality of Ralph Lauren's Polo franchise, recognition of the Polo player logo enhances the status of those who can afford his more expensive lines of clothing.

SIGNATURE BRANDS. A premium marketer typically cannot grow by introducing a mainstream brand under a different name. Premium marketers lack the resources to invest in developing such new franchises. In addition, the interest of mainstream distribution channels is in the existing premium brand rather than some new brand with no established consumer appeal. Faced with these circumstances, the premium marketer may compromise by introducing a signature brand (for example, Zips sneakers by Stride Rite). The objective is to exploit the halo benefits of the premium name while minimizing possible image damage.

LICENSING.   Rather than growing by pushing down the price pyramid in the product-markets where they currently operate, premium marketers and designers such as Yves St. Laurent are increasingly licensing use of their brand names to premium manufacturers in other product categories. As long as quality control can be maintained so that the licensed products reinforce rather than detract from the brand image, the premium marketer can grow laterally rather than vertically and not jeopardize the exclusivity of its franchise.[3]

GLOBAL MARKETING.   A global growth approach is similar to the previous strategy. The premium marketer targets the same premium segments in international markets that it currently targets in the domestic market. In many product-markets, increasing international travel and communications have led to a convergence across international boundaries in consumer values and their definitions of what is premium.[4] This convergence is often more evident in the premium than in the mainstream segment of product-markets. The size of the premium segment for Dupont cigarette lighters, which cost more than $300, may not be especially attractive in any one national market, but the global aggregate of multiple national premium segments may well be.

RETAIL OUTLETS.   Many premium marketers offer consumers a multiple product line of premium-quality items that represent a complete lifestyle concept. Sales growth is achieved by adding new products under the concept umbrella.

Often, however, the premium marketer finds that its product line is not fully presented or properly merchandised at the point-of-sale, no matter how carefully the retail outlets are selected. A premium product can easily lose its image for quality if it is lost among mainstream brands on a cluttered shelf. Hence, forward integration becomes a vehicle for the premium marketer to achieve both sales growth and merchandising control.

Many marketers of psychically grounded premium products—for example, Polo fashions, Haagen-Dazs, and Crabtree and Evelyn—are placing greater emphasis on establishing specialty stores dedicated exclusively to the sale of their own product lines and the lifestyle concepts associated with them. Such stores also act as advertising vehicles and boost sales of a premium marketer's products through other, nonexclusive channels.

STAYING ON TOP

What actions can the established premium marketer take to defend and solidify its niche? Obviously, it is necessary to establish a powerful, communicable, and defensible comparative advantage. In addition, several prescriptions may be helpful.

- *Pursue an internally consistent marketing strategy.* Premium marketers must ensure that all elements of the marketing mix—premium-quality product and positioning, premium pricing, selective distribution, and selective communications—are continually in concert.

- *Maintain quality leadership.* The premium marketer must closely monitor the meaning of "premium" to consumers in its target segments and beyond. The marketer must strive to ensure that "premium" continues to be defined on criteria that enable it to stay on top. However, to defend its position, the premium marketer must constantly challenge itself to improve the quality of its products. Mere exclusivity without quality leadership is a recipe for failure.

- *Cultivate a heritage.* Although few Reebok athletic shoes are now manufactured in the United Kingdom, part of the firm's advertising and public relations campaign focuses on the British founder of the company and the values of technical excellence and quality manufacture that he brought to the design and workmanship of Reebok shoes.

- *Develop quality indicators.* Performance warranties, competitive awards, expensive packaging, and brand logos are increasingly being used by actual and aspiring premium marketers to enhance the quality image of their brands. In an effort to upgrade its mainstream image, Gallo is advertising the awards its wines have received from connoisseurs and claims to offer "all the best a wine can be."

A NOTE OF CAUTION

Interest in the premium segments of most product-markets is likely to continue. Attracted by higher unit margins and the promise of greater strategic flexibility, mainstream marketers will seek to penetrate and grow the premium segment. For them, the key issue is not *whether* to enter but *how* to enter in order to succeed.

Their efforts will place established premium marketers under pressure. Some will not be able to defend their niches and will fade from view or be acquired. Others will seek growth in ways that do not jeopardize their established brand images. Some may trade down on the grounds that taking the offensive against the mainstream marketer is the best form of defense, even though this will leave them vulnerable at the high end of the market pyramid to the entry of superpremium brands.

One important caveat is in order. Marketers should be wary of devoting too much attention to the premium segment at the expense of other emerging segments (for example, retired persons) that may offer greater sales and profit potential. Just because they themselves are among the mere 3% of U.S. households in 1985 with incomes over $75,000, marketing decision makers may be tempted to attribute more importance to the premium segment than it deserves. Too many marketing executives look in their mirrors and think they see America.

If marketers become narrowly focused, marketing itself will be in danger of becoming a niche phenomenon. Satisfying the needs of the mass market will then be conceded to manufacturing-driven low-cost producers, Japanese and Korean manufacturers, and mass retailers (like

WalMart) who are close enough to the marketplace to develop appealing private-label products that will erode brand franchises even further.

If premium marketing becomes too glamorous and attracts a disproportionate share of our best marketing talent, the average American consumer will be the loser.

Three

Global Marketing

In the best of all possible worlds, marketers would only have to come up with a great product and a convincing marketing program and they would have a worldwide winner. But despite the obvious economies and efficiencies they could gain with a standard product and program, many managers fear that global marketing, as popularly defined, is too extreme to be practical. Because customers and competitive conditions differ across countries or because powerful local managers will not stand for centralized decision making, they argue, global marketing just won't work.

Of course, global marketing has its pitfalls, but it can also yield impressive advantages. Standardizing products can lower operating costs. Even more important, effective coordination can exploit a company's best product and marketing ideas.

Too often, executives view global marketing as an either/or proposition—either full standardization or local control. But when a global approach can fall anywhere on a spectrum from tight worldwide coordination on programming details to loose agreement on a product idea, why the extreme view? In applying the global marketing concept and making it work, flexibility is essential. Managers need to tailor the approach they use to each element of the business system and marketing program. For example, a manufacturer might market the same product under different brand names in different countries or market the same brands using different product formulas.

The big issue today is not whether to go global but how to tailor the global marketing concept to fit each business and how to make it work. In this chapter, we will first provide a framework to help managers think about how they should structure the different areas of the marketing function as the business shifts to a global approach. We will then show how companies we have studied are tackling the implementation challenges of global marketing.

HOW FAR TO GO

How far a company can move toward global marketing depends a lot on its evolution and traditions. Consider these two examples:

- Although the Coca-Cola Company had conducted some international business before 1940, it gained true global recognition during World War II, as Coke bottling plants followed the march of U.S. troops around the world. Management in Atlanta made all strategic decisions then—and still does now, as Coca-Cola applies global marketing principles, for example, to the worldwide introduction of Diet Coke. The brand name, concentrate formula, positioning, and advertising theme are virtually standard worldwide, but the artificial sweetener and packaging differ across countries. Local managers are responsible for sales and distribution programs, which they run in conjunction with local bottlers.

- The Nestlé approach also has its roots in history. To avoid distribution disruptions caused by wars in Europe, to ease rapid worldwide expansion, and to respond to local consumer needs,

Nestlé granted its local managers considerable autonomy from the outset. While the local managers still retain much of that decision-making power today, Nestlé headquarters at Vevey has grown in importance. Nestlé has transferred to its central marketing staff many former local managers who had succeeded in their local Nestlé businesses and who now influence country executives to accept standard new product and marketing ideas. The trend seems to be toward tighter marketing coordination.

To conclude that Coca-Cola is a global marketer and Nestlé is not would be simplistic. In Figure 3.1, we assess program adaptation or standardization levels for each company's business functions, products, marketing mix elements, and countries. Each company has tailored its individual approach. Furthermore, as Figure 3.1 cannot show, the situations are not static. Readers can themselves evaluate their own *current* and *desired* levels of program adaptation or standardization on these four dimensions. The gap between the two levels is the implementation challenge. The size of the gap—and the urgency with which it must be closed—will depend on a company's strategy and financial performance, competitive pressures, technological change, and converging consumer values.

Four Dimensions of Global Marketing

Let us now look at the issues that arise when executives consider the four dimensions shown in Figure 3.1 in light of the degree of standardization or adaptation that is appropriate.

Business Functions

A company's approach to global marketing depends, first, on its overall business strategy. In many multinationals, some functional areas have greater program standardization than others. Headquarters often controls manufacturing, finance, and R&D, while the local managers make the marketing decisions. Marketing is usually one of the last functions to be

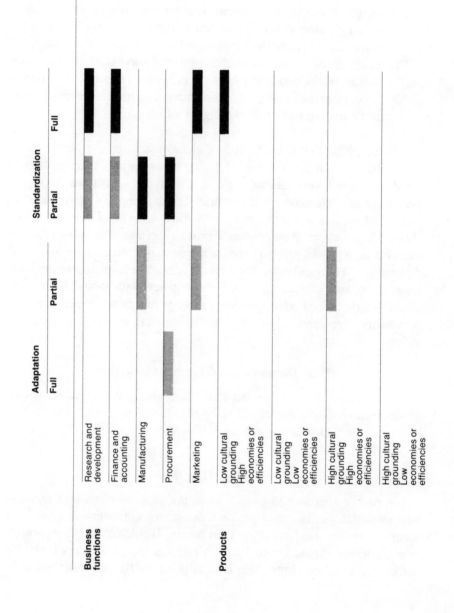

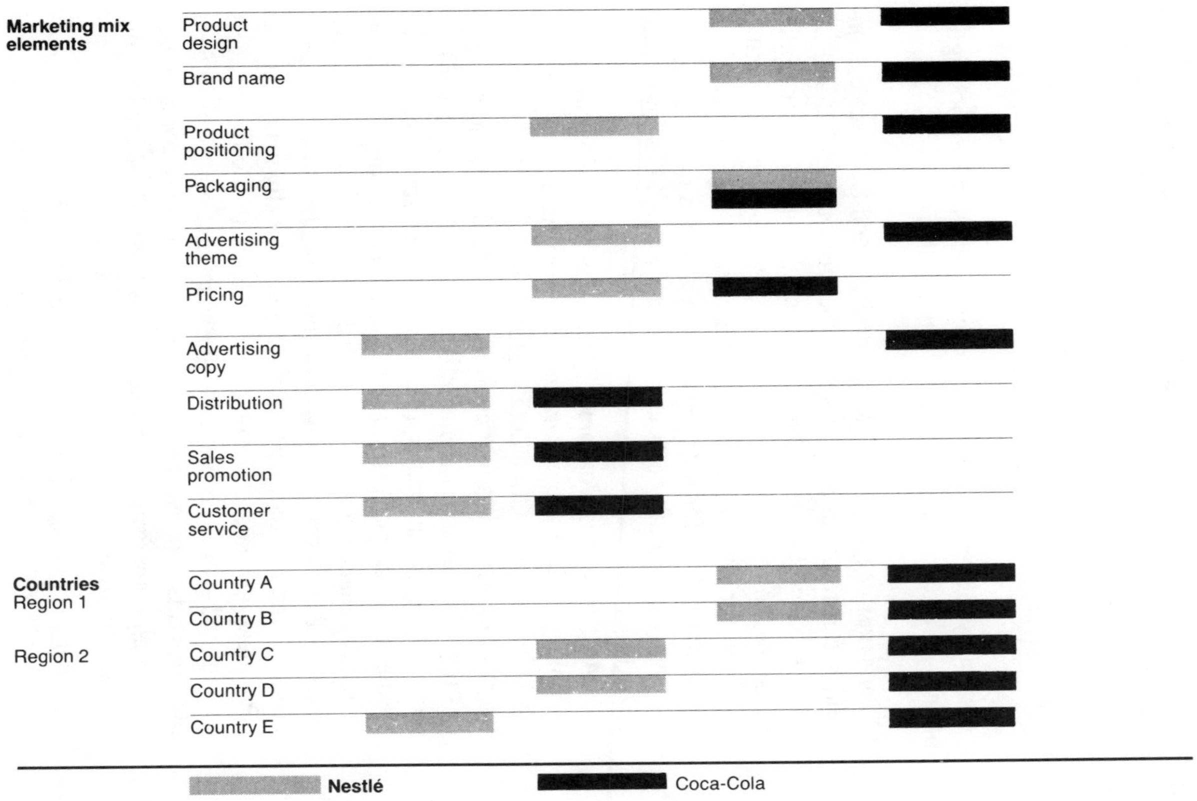

Marketing mix elements

Product design
Brand name
Product positioning
Packaging
Advertising theme
Pricing
Advertising copy
Distribution
Sales promotion
Customer service

Countries

Region 1
Country A
Country B

Region 2
Country C
Country D
Country E

Nestlé Coca-Cola

Figure 3.1. Global Marketing Planning Matrix: How Far to Go.

centrally directed. Partly because product quality and accounting data are easier to measure than marketing effectiveness, standardization can be greater in production and finance.

Products

Products that enjoy high-scale economies or efficiencies and are not highly culture-bound are easier to market globally than others.

(1) *Economies or efficiencies.* Manufacturing and R&D scale economies can result in a price spread between the global and the local product that is too great for even the most culture-bound consumer to resist. In addition, management often has neither the time nor the R&D resources to adapt products to each country. The markets for high-tech products like computers are not only very competitive but also affected by rapid technological change.

Most packaged consumer goods are less susceptible than durable good like televisions and cars to manufacturing or even R&D economies. Coca-Cola's global policy and Nestlé's interest in tighter marketing coordination are driven largely by a desire to capitalize on the marketing ideas their managers around the world generate rather than by potential scale economies. Nestlé, for example, manufactures its packaged soups in dozens of locally managed plants around the world, with some transference of engineering know-how through a headquarters staff. Products and marketing programs are also locally managed, but new ideas are aggressively transferred, with local managers encouraged—or even prodded—to adapt and use them in their own markets. For Nestlé, global marketing does not so much yield high manufacturing economies as high efficiency in using scarce new ideas.

(2) *Cultural grounding.* Consumer products used in the home—like Nestlé's soups and frozen foods—are often more culture-

bound than products used outside the home such as automobiles and credit cards, and industrial products are inherently less culture-bound than consumer products. (Products like personal computers, for example, are often marketed on the basis of performance benefits that share a common technical language worldwide.) Experience also suggests that products will be less culture-bound if they are used by young people whose cultural norms are not ingrained, people who travel in different countries, and ego-driven consumers who can be appealed to through myths and fantasies shared across cultures.

Figure 3.1 lists four combinations of the scale economy and cultural grounding variables in order of their susceptibility to global marketing. Managers shouldn't be bound by any matrix, however; they should find creative ways to prepare a product for global marketing. If a manufacturer develops a new version of a seemingly culture-bound product that is based on new capital-intensive technology and generates superior performance benefits, it may well be possible to introduce it on a standard basis worldwide. Procter & Gamble developed Pampers disposable diapers as a global brand in a product category that intuition would say was culture-bound.

Marketing Mix Elements

Few consumer goods companies go so far as to market the same products using the same marketing program worldwide. And those that do, like Lego, the Danish manufacturer of construction toys, often distribute their products through sales companies rather than full-fledged marketing subsidiaries.

For most products, the appropriate degree of standardization varies from one element of the marketing mix to another. Strategic elements like product positioning are more easily standardized than execution-sensitive elements like sales promotion. In addition, when headquarters believes it has identified a superior marketing idea, whether it be a package design, a brand name, or an advertising copy concept, the pressure to standardize increases.

Marketing can usually contribute to scale economies most significantly by creating a standard product design that will sell worldwide, permitting savings through globalized production. In addition, scale economies in marketing programming can be achieved through standard commercial executions and copy concepts. McCann-Erickson claims to have saved $90 million in production costs over 20 years by producing worldwide Coca-Cola commercials. To ensure that they have enough attention-getting power to overcome their foreign origins, however, marketers often have to make worldwide commercials expensive productions.

To compensate local management for having to accept a standard product and to fit the core product to each local market, some companies allow local managers to adapt those marketing mix elements that aren't subject to significant scale economies. On the other hand, local managers are more likely to accept a standard concept for those elements of the marketing mix that are less important and, ironically, often not susceptible to scale economies. Overall, then, the driving factor in moving toward global marketing should be the efficient worldwide use of good marketing ideas rather than any scale economies from standardization.

In judging how far to go in standardizing elements of the marketing mix, managers must also be mindful of the interactions among them. For example, when a product with the same brand name is sold in different countries, it can be difficult and sometimes impossible to sell them at different prices.

Countries

How far a decentralized multinational wishes to pursue global marketing will often vary from one country to another. Naturally, headquarters is likely to become more involved in marketing decisions in countries where performance is poor. But performance aside, small markets depend more on headquarters assistance than large markets. Because a standard marketing program is superior in quality to what local executives, even with the benefit of local market knowledge, could develop themselves, they may welcome it.

Large markets with strong local managements are less willing to accept global programs. Yet these are the markets that often account for most of the company's investment. To secure their acceptance, headquarters should make standard marketing programs reflect the needs of large rather than small markets. Small markets, being more tolerant of deviations from what would be locally appropriate, are less likely to resist a standard program.

As we've seen, Coca-Cola takes the same approach in all markets. Nestlé varies its approach in different countries depending on the strength of its market presence and each country's need for assistance. In completing the Figure 3.1 planning matrix, management may decide that it can sensibly group countries by region or by stage of market development.

TOO FAR TOO FAST

Once managers have decided how global they want their marketing program to be, they must make the transition. Debates over the size of the gap between present and desired positions and the speed with which it must be closed will often pit the field against headquarters. Such conflict is most likely to arise in companies where the reason for change is not apparent or the country managers have had a lot of autonomy. Casualties can occur on both sides:

- Because Black & Decker dominated the European consumer power tool market, many of the company's European managers could not see that a more centrally directed global marketing approach was needed as a defense against imminent Japanese competition. To make his point, the CEO had to replace several key European executives.
- In 1982, the Parker Pen Company, forced by competition and a weakening financial position to lower costs, more than halved its

number of plants and pen styles worldwide. Parker's overseas subsidiary managers accepted these changes but, when pressed to implement standardized advertising and packaging, they dug in their heels. In 1985, Parker ended its much heralded global marketing campaign. Several senior headquarters managers left the company.

If management is not careful, moving too far too fast toward global marketing can trigger painful consequences. First, subsidiary managers who joined the company because of its apparent commitment to local autonomy and to adapting its products to the local environment may become disenchanted. When poorly implemented, global marketing can make the local country manager's job less strategic. Second, disenchantment may reinforce not-invented-here attitudes that lead to game playing. For instance, some local managers may try bargaining with headquarters, trading the speed with which they will accept and implement the standard programs for additional budget assistance. In addition, local managers competing for resources and autonomy may devote too much attention to second-guessing headquarters' "hot buttons." Eventually the good managers may leave, and less competent people who lack the initiative of their predecessors may replace them.

A vicious circle can develop. Feeling compelled to review local performance more closely, headquarters may tighten its controls and reduce resources without adjusting its expectations of local managers. Meanwhile, local managers trying to gain approval of applications for deviations from standard marketing programs are being frustrated. The expanding headquarters bureaucracy and associated overhead costs reduce the speed with which the locals can respond to local opportunities and competitive actions. Slow response time is an especially serious problem with products for which barriers to entry for local competitors are low.

In this kind of system, weak, insecure local managers can become dependent on headquarters for operational assistance. They will want headquarters to assume the financial risks for new product launches and welcome the prepackaged marketing programs. If performance falls short of headquarters' expectations, the local management can always blame the failure on the quality of operational assistance or on the standard marketing program. The local manager who has clear autonomy and profit-and-loss responsibility cannot hide behind such excuses.

If headquarters or regions assume much of the strategic burden, managers in overseas subsidiaries may think only about short-term sales. This focus will diminish their ability to monitor and communicate to headquarters any changes in local competitors' strategic directions. When their responsibilities shift from strategy to execution, their ideas will become less exciting. If the field has traditionally been as important a source of new product ideas as the central R&D laboratory, the company may find itself short of the grassroots creative thinking and marketing research information that R&D needs. The fruitful dialogue that characterizes a relationship between equal partners will no longer flourish.

HOW TO GET THERE

When thinking about closing the gap between present and desired positions, most executives of decentralized multinationals want to accommodate their current organizational structures. They rightly view their subsidiaries and the managers who run them as important competitive strengths. They generally do not wish to transform these organizations into mere sales and distribution agencies.

How then in moving toward global marketing can headquarters build rather than jeopardize relationships, stimulate rather than demoralize local managers? The answer is to focus on means as much as ends, to examine the relationship between the home office and the field, and to ask what level of headquarters intervention for each business function, product, marketing mix element, and country is necessary to close the gap in each.

As Figure 3.2 indicates, headquarters can intervene at five points, ranging from informing to directing. The five intervention levels are

	Informing	Persuading	Coordinating	Approving	Directing
Business functions					
Research and development					
Finance and accounting					
Manufacturing					
Procurement					
Marketing					
Products					
Low cultural grounding High economies or efficiencies					
Low cultural grounding Low economies or efficiencies					
High cultural grounding High economies or efficiencies					
High cultural grounding Low economies or efficiencies					

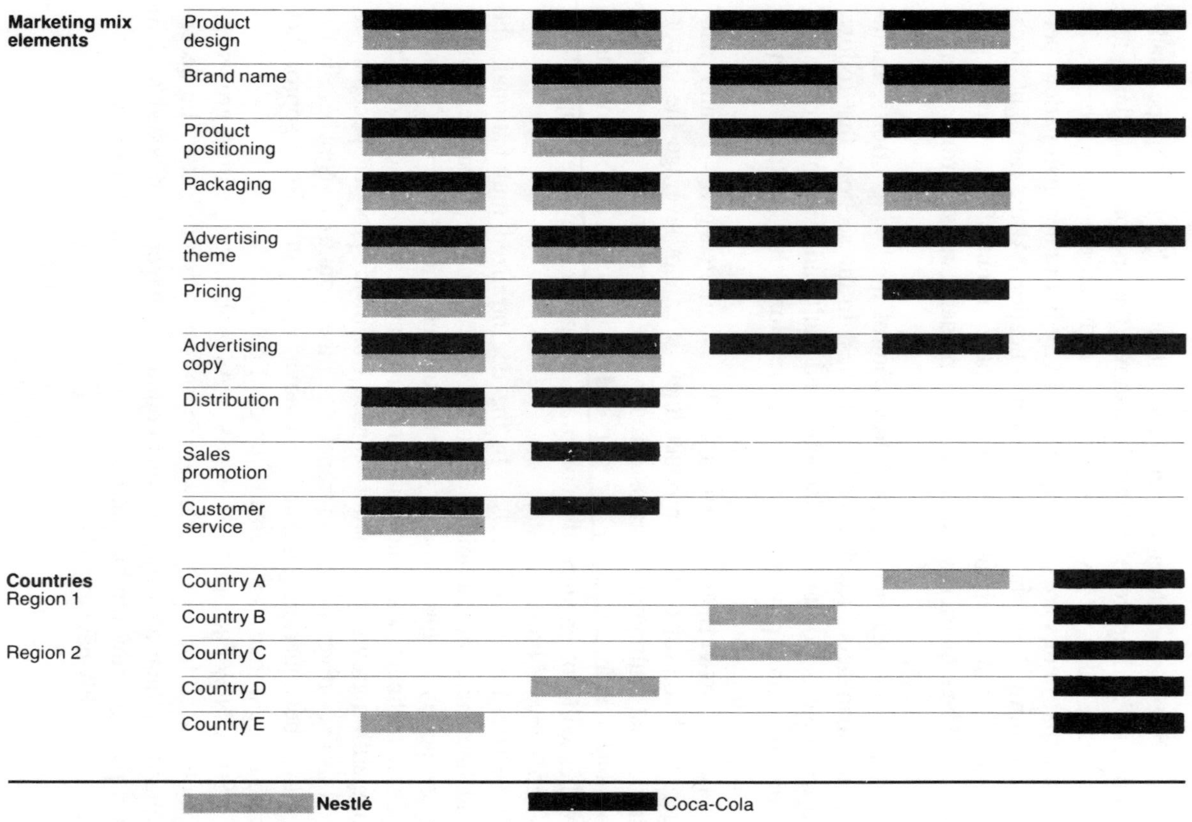

Marketing mix elements

Product design

Brand name

Product positioning

Packaging

Advertising theme

Pricing

Advertising copy

Distribution

Sales promotion

Customer service

Countries

Region 1

Country A

Country B

Country C

Region 2

Country D

Country E

Nestlé   Coca-Cola

Figure 3.2. Global Marketing Planning Matrix: How to Get There.

cumulative; for headquarters to direct, it must also inform, persuade, coordinate, and approve. Figure 3.2 shows the approaches Atlanta and Vevey have taken. Moving from left to right on the figure, the reader can see that things are done increasingly by fiat rather than patient persuasion, through discipline rather than education. At the far right, local subsidiaries cannot choose whether to opt in or out of a marketing program, and headquarters views its country managers as subordinates rather than customers.

When the local managers tightly control marketing efforts, multinational managers face three critical issues. In the sections that follow, we will take a look at how decentralized multinationals are working to correct the three problems as they move along the spectrum from informing to directing.

INCONSISTENT BRAND IDENTITIES. If headquarters gives country managers total control of their product lines, it cannot leverage the opportunities that multinational status gives it. The increasing degree to which consumers in one country are exposed to the company's products in another will not enhance the corporate image or brand development in the consumers' home country.

LIMITED PRODUCT FOCUS. In the decentralized multinational, the field line manager's ambition is to become a country manager, which means acquiring multiproduct and multifunction experience. Yet as the pace of technological innovation increases and the likelihood of global competition grows, multinationals need worldwide product specialists as well as executives willing to transfer to other countries. Nowhere is the need for headquarters guidance on innovative organizational approaches more evident than in the area of product policy.

SLOW NEW PRODUCT LAUNCHES. As global competition grows, so does the need for rapid worldwide rollouts of new products. The decentralized multinational that permits country managers to proceed at their own pace on new product introductions may be at a competitive disadvantage in this new environment.

Word of Mouth

The least threatening, loosest, and therefore easiest approach to global marketing is for headquarters to encourage the transfer of information between it and its country managers. Since good ideas are often a company's scarcest resource, headquarters efforts to encourage and reward their generation, dissemination, and application in the field will build both relationships and profits. Following are two examples:

- Nestlé publishes quarterly marketing newsletters that report recent product introductions and programming innovations. In this way, each subsidiary can learn quickly about and assess the ideas of others. (The best newsletters are written as if country organizations were talking to each other rather than as if headquarters were talking down to the field.)

- Johnson Wax holds periodic meetings of all marketing directors at corporate headquarters twice a year to build global esprit de corps and to encourage the sharing of new ideas.

By making the transfer of information easy, a multinational leverages the ideas of its staff and spreads organizational values. Headquarters has to be careful, however, that the information it is passing on is useful. It may focus on updating local managers about new products, when what they mainly want is information on the most tactical and country-specific elements of the marketing mix. For example, the concentration of the grocery trade is much higher in the United Kingdom and Canada than it is in the United States. In this case, managers in the United States can learn from British and Canadian country managers about how to deal with the pressures for extra merchandising support that result when a few powerful retailers control a large percentage of sales. Likewise, marketers in countries with restrictions on mass media advertising have developed sophisticated point-of-purchase merchandising skills that could be useful to managers in other countries.

By itself, however, information sharing is often insufficient to help local executives meet the competitive challenges of global marketing.

Friendly Persuasion

Persuasion is a first step managers can take to deal with the three problems we have outlined. Any systematic headquarters effort to influence local managers to apply standardized approaches or introduce new global products while the latter retain their decision-making authority is a persuasion approach.

Unilever and CPC International, for example, employ world-class advertising and marketing research staff at headquarters. Not critics but coaches, these specialists review the subsidiaries' work and try to upgrade the technical skills of local marketing departments. They frequently visit the field to disseminate new concepts, frameworks, and techniques, and to respond to problems that local management raises. (It helps to build trust if headquarters can send out the same staff specialists for several years.)

Often, when the headquarters of a decentralized multinational identifies or develops a new product, it has to persuade the country manager in a so-called prime-mover market to invest in the launch. A successful launch in the prime-mover market will, in turn, persuade other country managers to introduce the product. The prime-mover market is usually selected according to criteria including the commitment of local management, the probabilities of success, the credibility with which a success would be regarded by managers in other countries, and its perceived transferability.

Persuasion, however, has its limitations. Two problems recur with the prime-mover approach. First, by adopting a wait-and-see attitude, country managers can easily turn down requests to be prime-mover markets on the grounds of insufficient resources. Since the country managers in the prime-mover markets have to risk their resources to launch the new products, they are likely to tailor the product and marketing programs to their own markets rather than to global markets. Second, if there are more new products waiting to be launched than there are prime-mover markets to launch them, headquarters product specialists are likely to give in to a country manager's demands for local tailoring. But because of the need for readaptation in each case, the tailoring may delay rollouts in other markets and allow competitors to preempt the product. In the end, management may sacrifice long-term worldwide profits to maximize short-term profits in a few countries.

Marketing to the Same Drummer

To overcome the limits of persuasion, many multinationals are coordinating their marketing programs, whereby headquarters has a structured role in both decision making and performance evaluation that is far more influential than person-to-person persuasion. Often using a matrix or team approach, headquarters shares with country managers the responsibility and authority for programming and personnel decisions.

Nestlé locates product directors as well as support groups at headquarters. Together they develop long-term strategies for each product category on a worldwide basis, coordinate worldwide market research, spot new product opportunities, spark the field launch of new products, advise the field on how headquarters will evaluate new product proposals, and spread the word on new products' performance so that other countries will be motivated to launch them. Even though the product directors are staff executives with no line authority, because they have all been successful line managers in the field, they have great credibility and influence.

Country managers who cooperate with a product director can quickly become heroes if they successfully implement a new idea. On the other hand, while a country manager can reject a product director's advice, headquarters will closely monitor his or her performance with an alternative program. In addition, within the product category in which they specialize, the directors have influence on line management appointments in the field. Local managers thus have to be concerned about their relationships with headquarters.

Some companies assign promising local managers to other countries and require would-be local managers to take a tour of duty at head-quarters. But such personnel transfer programs may run into barriers. First, many capable local nationals may not be interested in working outside their countries of origin. Second, powerful local managers are often unwilling to give up their best people to other country assignments. Third, immigration regulations and foreign service relocation costs are burdensome. Fourth, if transferees from the field have to take a demotion to work at headquarters, the costs in ill will often exceed any gains in cross-fertilization of ideas. If management can resolve these problems, however, it will find that creating an international career path is one of the most effective ways to develop a global perspective in local managers.

To enable their regional general managers to work alongside the worldwide product directors, several companies have moved them from the field to the head office. More and more companies require regional managers to reach sales and profit targets for each product as well as for each country within their regions. In the field, regional managers often focus on representing the views of individual countries to headquarters, but at headquarters they become more concerned with ensuring that the country managers are correctly implementing corporatewide policies.

Recently, Fiat and Philips N.V., among others, consolidated their worldwide advertising into a single agency. Their objectives are to make each product's advertising more consistent around the world and to make it easier to transfer ideas and information among local agency offices, country organizations, and headquarters. Use of a single agency (especially one that bills all advertising expenditures worldwide) also symbolizes a commitment to global marketing and more centralized control. Multinationals should not, however, use their agencies as Trojan horses for greater standardization. An undercover operation is likely to jeopardize agency-client relations at the country level.

While working to achieve global coordination, some companies are also trying to tighten coordination in particular regions:

- Kodak recently experimented by consolidating 17 worldwide product line managers at corporate headquarters. In addition, the company made marketing directors in some countries responsible for a line of business in a region as well as for sales of all Kodak products in their own countries. Despite these new appointments, country managers still retain profit-and-loss responsibility for their own markets.

Whether a matrix approach such as this broadens perspectives rather than increases tension and confusion depends heavily on the corporation's cohesiveness. Such an organizational change can clearly communicate top management's strategic direction, but headquarters needs to do a persuasive selling job to the field if it is to succeed.

- Procter & Gamble has established so-called Euro Brand teams that analyze opportunities for greater product and marketing program standardization. Chaired by the brand manager from a "lead country," each team includes brand managers from other European subsidiaries that market the brand, managers from P&G's European technical center, and one of P&G's three European division managers, each of whom is responsible for a portfolio of brands as well as for a group of countries. Concerns that the larger subsidiaries would dominate the teams and that decision making would either be paralyzed or produce "lowest common denominator" results have proved groundless.

Stamped and Approved

By coordinating programs with the field, headquarters can balance the company's local and global perspectives. Even a decentralized multinational may decide, however, that to protect or exploit some corporate asset, the center of gravity for certain elements of the marketing program should be at headquarters. In such cases, management has two options: it can send clear directives to its local managers or permit them to develop their own programs within specified parameters and subject to headquarters approval. With a properly managed approval process, a multinational can exert effective control without unduly dampening the country manager's decision-making responsibility and creativity.

Procter & Gamble recently developed a new sanitary napkin, and P&G International designated certain countries in different geographic regions as test markets. The product, brand name, positioning, and package design were standardized globally. P&G International did, however, invite local managers to suggest how the global program could be improved and how the nonglobal elements of the marketing program should be adapted in their markets. It approved changes in several markets. Moreover, local managers developed valuable ideas on such programming specifics as sampling and couponing techniques that were used in all other countries, including the United States.

Nestlé views its brand names as a major corporate asset. As a result, it requires all brands sold in all countries to be registered in the home country of Switzerland. While the ostensible reason for this requirement is legal protection, the effect is that any product developed in the field has to be approved by Vevey. The head office has also developed detailed guidelines that suggest rather than mandate how brand names and logos should appear on packaging and in advertising worldwide (with exceptions subject to its approval). Thus the country manager's control over the content of advertising is not compromised, and the company achieves a reasonably consistent presentation of its names and logos worldwide.

Doing It the Headquarters Way

Multinationals that direct local managers' marketing programs usually do so out of a sense of urgency. The motive may be to ensure either that a new product is introduced rapidly around the world before the competition can respond or that every manager fully and faithfully exploits a valuable marketing idea. Sometimes direction is needed to prove that global marketing can work. Once management makes the point, a more participative approach is feasible.

In 1979, one of Henkel's worldwide marketing directors wanted to extend the successful Sista line of do-it-yourself sealants from Germany to other European countries where the markets were underdeveloped and disorganized as had once been the case in Germany. A European headquarters project team visited the markets and then developed a standard marketing program. The country managers, however, objected. Since the market potential in each country was small, they said, they did not have the time or resources to launch Sista.

The project team countered that by capitalizing on potential scale economies, its pan-European marketing and manufacturing programs would be superior to any programs the subsidiaries could develop by themselves. Furthermore, it maintained, the already developed pan-European program was available off the shelf. The European sales manager, who was a project team member, discovered that the salespeople as well as tradespeople in the target countries were much more enthusiastic about the proposed program than the field marketing managers. So management devised a special lure for the managers. The project team offered to subsidize the first-year advertising and promotion expenditures of countries launching Sista. Six countries agreed. To ensure their commitment now that their financial risk had been reduced, the sales manager invited each accepting country manager to nominate a member to the project team to develop the final program details.

By 1982, the Sista line was sold in 52 countries using a standard marketing program. The Sista launch was especially challenging because it involved the extension of a product and program already developed for a single market. The success of the Sista launch made Henkel's field managers much more receptive to global marketing programs for subsequent new products.

MOTIVATING THE FIELD

Taking into account the nature of their products and markets, their organizational structures, and their cultures and traditions, multinationals have to decide which approach or combination of approaches, from informing to directing, will best answer their strategic objectives. Multinational managers must realize, however, that local managers are likely to resist any precipitate move toward increased headquarters direction. A quick shift could lower their motivation and performance.

Any erosion in marketing decision making associated with global marketing will probably be less upsetting for country managers who have not risen through the line marketing function. For example, John Deere's European headquarters has developed advertising for its European country managers for more than a decade. The country managers have not objected. Most are not marketing specialists and do not see advertising as key to the success of their operations. But for country managers who view control of marketing decision making as central to their operational success, the transition will often be harder. Headquarters needs to give the field time to adjust to the new decision-making processes that multi-country brand teams and other new organizational structures require. Yet management must recognize that even with a one- or two-year transition period, some turnover among field personnel is inevitable. As one German headquarters executive commented, "Those managers in the field who can't adapt to a more global approach will have to leave and run local breweries."

Here are five suggestions on how to motivate and retain talented country managers when making the shift to global marketing:

(1) Encourage field managers to generate ideas. This is especially important when R&D efforts are centrally directed. Use the best ideas from the field in global marketing programs (and give recognition to the local managers who came up with them). Unilever's South African subsidiary developed Impulse body spray, now a global brand. R.J. Reynolds revitalized Camel as a global brand after the German subsidiary came up with a successful and transferable positioning and copy strategy.

(2) Ensure that the field participates in the development of the marketing strategies and programs for global brands. A bottom-up rather than top-down approach will foster greater commitment and produce superior program execution at the country level. As we have seen, when P&G International introduced its san-

itary napkin as a global brand, it permitted local managers to make some adjustments in areas that were not seen as core to the program, such as couponing and sales promotion. More important, it encouraged them to suggest changes in features of the core global program.

(3) Maintain a product portfolio that includes, where scale economies permit, local as well as regional and global brands. While Philip Morris's and Seagram's country managers and their local advertising agencies are required to implement standard programs for each company's global brands, the managers retain full responsibility for the marketing programs of their locally distributed brands. Seagram motivates its country managers to stay interested in the global brands by allocating development funds to support local marketing efforts on these brands and by circulating monthly reports that summarize market performance data by brand and country.

(4) Allow country managers continued control of their marketing budgets so they can respond to local consumer needs and counter local competition. When British Airways headquarters launched its £13 million global advertising campaign, it left intact the £18 million worth of tactical advertising budgets that country managers used to promote fares, destinations, and tour packages specific to their markets. Because most of the country managers had exhausted their previous year's tactical budgets and were anxious for further advertising support, they were receptive to the global campaign even though it was centrally directed.

(5) Emphasize the general management responsibilities of country managers that extend beyond the marketing function. Country managers who have risen through the line marketing function often do not spend enough time on local manufacturing operations, industrial relations, and government affairs. Global marketing programs can free them to focus on and develop their skills in these other areas.

Four

Local Marketing

M arketers of national brands of consumer goods and services are
increasingly being urged to adopt local marketing. Local marketing
means the tailoring of one or more aspects of a national marketing program, or the use of supplementary programs, to meet local consumer or
trade needs. This tailoring can occur at various levels of disaggregation
on both a geographic basis (a different program for a region, a city, or
zip code) or on a trade account basis (a different program for a particular
retail chain, a division of the chain, or an individual store).

Local marketing is nothing new. The product formulas for national
brands of coffee have long been tailored to regional tastes. Heavier advertising and promotion expenditures as a percentage of sales have often
been used to boost brand trial in low-category or brand-development
markets. Standard sales force workplans have frequently been adjusted
to combat regional brands that remain especially competitive in, for example, short shelf-life categories such as snack foods and cookies. New

products have regularly been rolled out on a region-by-region basis, with marketing programs adapted along the way to increase the odds of success.

Local marketing has been especially evident in service businesses. For example, fast food marketers like McDonald's have encouraged their franchisees to establish close ties with local communities through customized promotions that involve local media, sports teams, and charities. Convinced of the effectiveness of these local promotions, franchisees from automobile dealerships to fast food restaurants are increasingly challenging the percentage of their sales that the head office employs for national marketing programs.

Such moves are symptomatic of the current surge of interest in local marketing and the tendency toward a higher percentage of marketing budgets being allocated to local versus national programs. A 1987 Dechert-Hampe survey reported that 56% of consumer marketers had plans to implement regional marketing programs in 1988 and that 43% of those already involved in regional marketing planned to spend more than 20% of their marketing budgets on local marketing programs.[1] Recent examples include:

- Between 1985 and 1987, Frito Lay quadrupled the local marketing budgets set aside for its zone sales managers to allocate.[2]

- In 1987, Lever Brothers offered Surf detergent only in liquid form in northern United States where liquid detergents are more popular and only in powdered form in southern states.

- Airlines now regularly raise the bonus mileage offered to frequent fliers on routes where their competitive position is weak.

- Vons supermarket chain classifies its stores into five groups on the basis of demographic analyses of each one's patrons and adjusts its product assortments accordingly.[3]

- Automobile manufacturers, often in association with regional dealer networks, are developing special limited edition models to cater to regional tastes; targeting direct mail drops to zip codes with demographics that fit the profiles of likely purchasers of particular models; and adapting media mixes by region to reflect the lifestyles of prospective customers.[4]

In the past, local marketing has largely been seen as a necessary inconvenience, undertaken for defensive reasons. Today, however, excellence in local marketing is being viewed as a potential source of competitive advantage. In this chapter, we:

- Discuss the environmental trends that explain the emerging interest in local marketing and profile the product categories that are most affected.

- Identify the principal costs and risks that manufacturers must consider before implementing local marketing programs.

- Offer guidelines for developing and implementing a local marketing strategy that goes beyond an ad hoc collection of localized sales promotion events.

GROWING IMPORTANCE OF LOCAL MARKETING

Changes in the marketing environment are causing the growing interest in local marketing. First, consumer heterogeneity is more evident. The mass market has given way to a patchwork quilt of demographic, geographic, and lifestyle segments for which national programs just do not work as well. With a population growth rate of less than 1%, marketers are concentrating on adding value to specific segments through customizing their marketing programs as a way to differentiate themselves from competitors and boost their margins. Local marketing offers the advantages of bringing the marketer closer to the end consumer, facilitating feedback from the marketplace, and permitting more effective customization of the marketing program.

The same environmental trends are prompting retailers as well as manufacturers to pay more attention to market segmentation in general and local marketing in particular. New retail store formats from hypermarkets and warehouse stores to large convenience and specialty niche stores have emerged to serve the needs of an increasingly segmented consumer population. Growing trade segmentation means that producers are under pressure to tailor marketing programs by class of trade or according to the needs of individual key accounts. Serving classes of trade such as grocery retailing, where there are no truly national chains, where the industry structure varies by region, and where decentralization of decision making on product assortment and merchandising programs is increasing, inevitably demands more local marketing by manufacturers.

Trade pressure is a function of growing trade power. Concentration in many classes of trade is increasing, particularly when market shares are examined on a market-specific rather than national basis. The sophistication of retail management is improving as retailers learn to exploit the information power afforded by sales data collected by scanner systems at the point-of-sale. Sixty percent of grocery stores now have scanning equipment.[5] Falling data processing costs are further encouraging retailers to use scanner data to gain a competitive advantage by tailoring their assortments to the consumer needs in the trading area that each store serves; as this occurs, producers will find it harder to secure acceptance of their products and merchandising programs in all stores unless they too customize their marketing programs. As trade power grows, retailers are no longer merely responding to manufacturer promotions but are increasingly developing their own differentiated promotion programs and offering participation opportunities to the manufacturers. For manufacturer-initiated promotion offers to attract trade attention, they must increasingly be customized to local market and individual account needs.

Media audience fragmentation, like trade format proliferation, is a response to growing consumer segmentation. The prime time television audience that the three networks can command has fallen from 92% in 1979 to 77% today in the face of an ever-expanding and improving set of cable and broadcast alternatives.[6] The rate spread advantage of national over local media for equivalent exposures is diminishing. Spot advertising can now be purchased a year ahead and can therefore be more readily incorporated into brand media plans. Regional media buying agencies are helping national manufacturers make spot purchases more easily and cost efficiently. Not surprisingly, the growth of local advertising expenditures is outpacing national advertising expenditures.[7]

The growing importance of sales promotion (both trade and consumer promotion) versus advertising in most brand budgets both reflects and reinforces the trend toward local marketing. Sales promotions can be more readily localized, right down to the store level where, for example, in-store sampling and couponing programs for a new product can be executed in stores whose customers most closely match the manufacturer's target market. Sales promotion offers can also be mailed to households identified through sophisticated geodemographic computer programs that match zip code profiles to target consumers.[8] Likewise, the value and nature of offers presented in nationally distributed freestanding inserts can be customized by market. Finally, local media owners are sufficiently aware of the local marketing trend that they are providing opportunities, attractive rates, and executional capabilities to interested advertisers. Brand managers are discovering that taking advantage of these local marketing options can make it harder for national brand competitors to identify, match, and beat their advertising and promotion schedules than if they each have only a single national plan.

AFFECTED PRODUCTS

These trends are affecting all consumer goods and service marketers but certain nationally distributed products and services appear especially susceptible to local marketing. Their characteristics are as follows:

- They face significant, identifiable differences in consumer behavior, trade mix and needs, or relative competitive position from one market area to another.

- They are based on mature technologies and, as a result, the superiority of national brands over each other as well as over regional and store brands is limited, if it exists at all.

- They are high bulk-to-value products and are, therefore, less subject to cross-market diversion if offered at different prices in different markets. Hence, there is more regional marketing of tuna and pasta than of health and beauty aids.

Strong franchise brands are better candidates for local marketing, particularly in the area of consumer promotion. They enjoy the necessary dollar sales volume and margin structure to fund local programs and the additional managers needed to tailor their national programs to local needs. Ironically, the weak franchise brands that are more in need of the extra boost local marketing can give to secure trade support are less able to execute local programs.

COSTS AND RISKS

Managers of many consumer goods and services are embracing local marketing without fully understanding the costs and risks. There are four key concerns. First, the strategic implications of excessive local marketing must be recognized. Any manager of a national brand should be aware that the diversion of advertising and promotion funds to local marketing programs may dilute rather than reinforce the brand franchise, partly because the field salespeople who execute them typically have a shorter-term perspective than brand management. For example, Frito Lay, the only nationally distributed U.S. snack food manufacturer, should not jeopardize this unique advantage by over-emphasizing local marketing to compete against Borden Inc.'s network of eight regional brands.[9] National brand franchises must and can be defended in other ways besides local marketing; from cakes to cookies, experience shows that national brands can boost their market shares at the expense of less resource-rich regional brands and weaker national competitors by increasing either national marketing expenditures or the pace of new product development.

Second, adapting national marketing programs to local needs costs management time and effort that could be directed toward developing innovative, differentiated product features and thereby possibly contribute more to the long-term strength of national brand franchises. Local marketing demands additional management personnel when, today, most consumer marketers are facing a slow growth environment in which cost controls are assuming increasing importance. For example, Campbell Soup Company had to hire four new headquarters staff managers to communicate with 22 newly appointed regional brand sales managers.[10] In addition to more management time, local marketing is likely to increase the costs of market research and information systems needed to gather and process local market data and to evaluate local marketing efforts, particularly sales promotions. Advertising costs may also rise if national buying efficiencies cannot be fully exploited. As with any segmentation scheme, we must ask whether the extra costs of local marketing can be more than offset by additional sales and/or higher margins.

A third concern deals specifically with the customization of trade deal rates and merchandising programs. When a brand's market share differs across markets, there is good reason to offer higher deal rates in low-share markets where the brand's franchise is less well developed. However, a retail chain with stores in several markets could buy its entire needs of a brand in the market where the best deal was being offered. Thus, local trade promotion programs may encourage forward buying and diversion, reduce the accuracy of sales forecasts, and add to production and logistics costs in the form of additional capacity, emergency production runs, and extra safety stocks of inventory. Local marketing may, thereby, reinforce the power of larger distributors, further aggravating the pressure on manufacturers to provide customized local marketing programs.

A fourth, related, concern is legal in nature. Under the Robinson-Patman Act, a manufacturer must offer equivalent allowances to all distributors in a particular market area. While local marketing is perfectly legal, it encourages individual wholesalers and retailers to press their claims for customized treatment—for example, more generous allowance rates or the development of special merchandising programs—that may place manufacturers in potentially embarrassing situations.

DEVELOPING A STRATEGY

Notwithstanding these costs and risks are the strong environmental pressures for customizing elements of the marketing mix for particular regions, classes of trade, or key trade accounts. To arrive at a local marketing strategy, managers must first take into account three key decisions.

DECIDE WHAT TO LOCALIZE. Using a framework such as Table 4.1, managers can decide which elements of each product's marketing mix should be customized in response to consumer needs, trade demands, or competitive pressures. Typically, we would expect local customization to be more prevalent among the execution-sensitive and price-related mix elements such as trade and consumer promotion and expect more standardization on the strategic and image-related dimensions such as brand name and product positioning. Supporting this contention, the Dechert-Hampe survey reported that 80% of managers planned to regionalize trade promotion, 79% consumer promotion, and only 52% media advertising.[11]

DECIDE HOW FAR TO GO. While some cost-conscious companies will engage in only token local marketing as a defensive measure, others may decide to invest in local marketing as an offensive strategy. A breakdown of the latter's marketing expenditures as outlined in Table 4.2 is likely to reveal a higher proportion of funds allocated to customized programs on both the geographic and trade dimensions. A sampling (not to be considered representative) of the 1987 marketing budgets for three leading consumer packaged goods brands generated the average distribution of expenditures shown in Table 4.3.

Table 4.1.   CUSTOMIZATION OF A MARKETING PROGRAM

	NATIONAL STANDARDIZATION	*LOCAL CUSTOMIZATION*
PRODUCT FORMULATION		
PRODUCT POSITIONING		
PACKAGING		
BRAND NAME		
PRODUCT LINE		
ADVERTISING		
PRICING		
DISTRIBUTION		
CUSTOMER SERVICE		
SALES ORGANIZATION		
CONSUMER PROMOTION		
TRADE PROMOTION		

Table 4.2. ALLOCATION OF A MARKETING BUDGET

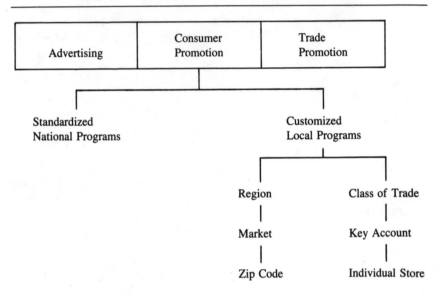

Two further comments on the marketing expenditure mix:

- Local consumer promotion expenditures are growing the fastest. While production economics demand that consumer promotions that involve a change in package size or content usually remain national in scope, manufacturers such as General Foods see local couponing and sampling offers as a way to shift funds from purely price-oriented trade promotions to vehicles that can deliver a brand benefit message as well as an economic incentive.[12] Retailer-initiated cooperative promotion and advertising programs are fueling this trend and blurring the traditional distinctions among advertising, consumer promotion, and trade promotion.

- The national-local mix for any brand will vary across regions depending on the unique demands of particular markets—though

Table 4.3.   AVERAGE 1987 BUDGET ALLOCATIONS FOR THREE BRANDS

	NATIONAL	*LOCAL*
ADVERTISING	23%	10%
CONSUMER PROMOTION	8%	7%
TRADE PROMOTION	37%	14%

brand management may attempt to cluster its markets and accounts to minimize the number of separate programs that have to be developed.

DECIDE HOW FAST TO GO.   The speed at which a company moves toward local marketing is a function of the strength of the environmental pressures outlined above, constraints imposed by the current organization structure, and the company's current financial performance. General Foods, for example, is taking a controlled experimental approach. General Foods has a headquarters staff director for local marketing, is testing a new local marketing strategy and organization in the Denver market, and is injecting more local marketing into its new product introduction plans.[13] In contrast, Campbell Soup Company has implemented a dramatic organization change, appointing 22 regional brand sales managers, to secure a competitive advantage by positioning itself to the trade as a leader in regional marketing.[14]

INCREASED SALES FORCE ROLE

Once these strategic decisions are taken, management can appropriately consider the marketing and sales organizations needed to implement the local marketing strategy. Consumer goods and services companies need a marketing/sales organization that represents three perspectives: product, geography, and the trade. Traditionally, brand management has represented the product dimension while the sales force has been organized geographically. With local marketing, the relative importance of the geographic dimension as reflected in the decision-making responsibility of the sales force should increase. While brand management should be able to plan local coupon drops from headquarters by matching zip code profiles with a brand's target consumers, field sales will need to develop even more new skills. Training will be needed to help regional sales managers develop and implement special event promotions with local trade accounts, use public relations to promote these events, and perhaps buy local advertising time and space. Greater complexity in the sales organization is also likely as companies explore combinations of direct salespeople, part-timers, and brokers to maximize their leverage in individual markets.

As a company embraces local marketing in the area of sales promotion, the marketing organization typically passes through three stages:

- *Stage 1.* All decisions on sales promotions are made centrally by brand management. All promotions are national in scope. There is minimal deviation from the promotion calendars planned by brand management.

- *Stage 2.* Sales promotion decisions continue to be made centrally by brand management. Some regional as well as national promotions are planned and evaluated by assistant brand managers, particularly within the larger brand groups. Brand management adjudicates sales force requests for additional and alternative promotion expenditures to meet unanticipated competitive activity and opportunities in specific markets. Sales merchandising managers at headquarters, each handling a different sales region, interface between brand and sales managements on such requests and are responsible for coordinating the promotion calendars for each region and product.

- *Stage 3*. Brand management sets national and local sales promotion budgets. Sales management is responsible for allocating each brand's local promotion budget to meet preagreed sales volume goals. The advantages of this approach are:

  The company can respond quickly to offers to participate in the vendor support programs proposed by retail accounts.

  Brand management need no longer be distracted by calls from the field seeking approvals of unscheduled promotion funds.

  Increased decision-making responsibility in the field motivates the sales force.

  Devolution of responsibility insulates headquarters from examining the legitimacy of every promotion offer under the Robinson-Patman Act.

If a company moves to Stage 3, it must consider basing evaluations of district and regional sales managers on profit delivery and accurate sales forecasting (which will be reflected in trade customer service levels) as well as on sales volume. Additional responsibility also means that higher caliber salespeople with new marketing skills and extra training will be required.

TRADE MARKETING

The marketing organizations of consumer goods and services companies can currently represent the interests of the trade in three ways: separate sales forces for particular classes of trade; proven salespeople appointed as key account managers to serve the needs of major customers and, where necessary, coordinate the sell-in efforts of several salespeople in multidivision companies; and the use of brokers when they have long-standing relationships with the trade and can achieve deeper account penetration than a direct sales force because of more frequent store coverage.

Given the increasing power and heterogeneity of the trade, these approaches may no longer be sufficient. Larger companies should consider adding a headquarters function focusing on the strategic aspects of trade marketing as an overlay to the existing brand management system because brand managers traditionally focus more on product and consumer issues rather than on the trade.[15] This might be accomplished by retraining existing personnel or, in large organizations, by creating a new department with the following responsibilities:

- Monitor and analyze trends in trade marketing and provide appropriate information to brand and sales managements.

- Develop business strategies for each class of trade and for certain key trade accounts and work with brand and sales managements to ensure their implementation.

- Evaluate the effectiveness of trade merchandising efforts and work up measures such as a store development index (similar to brand and category development indices) to do so.

- Develop value-added services for the sales force to offer trade accounts. Such services might include assistance in allocating shelf space in a product category according to direct product profit,[16] and multiple- or single-brand turnkey promotion programs that field sales can take off the shelf as needed.

- Serve as an information clearing house for creative promotion and merchandising programs developed in the field and for account management strategies and tactics, to minimize reinvention of the wheel.

- Advise on the setting of terms of trade (such as quantity discounts and backhaul allowances) on the basis of cost analyses, and work with the logistics and manufacturing departments to ensure customer service objectives are met.

- Assist in training programs to give field sales and brokers the marketing skills necessary to distinguish themselves from competition in the eyes of an increasingly sophisticated trade, and also to improve the sales skills and trade sensitivity of brand management.

- Encourage, through information dissemination and advocacy, a perception throughout the organization of the trade as a necessary partner to be successful.

After instituting a trade development function at headquarters, a company may also elect to retrain existing sales managers and/or appoint tactically oriented trade development managers in regional sales offices who would:

- Advise region managers on field sales or broker requests for incremental trade promotions in response to competitive activity or retailer offers to participate in their own promotion programs.

- Understand the merchandising strategies of key trade accounts in the region and develop custom promotion programs for them.

- Coordinate the promotion calendars for the company's products and trade accounts in the region and minimize the chances of competing accounts in a single market using the same promotion at the same time.

These trade development managers will need an unusual combination of strategic thinking and implementation skills. They will have to bring to their jobs the perspectives of field sales, brand management, and the trade. Not surprisingly, 75% of respondents to the Dechert-Hampe survey concluded that a new breed of manager was needed to handle local marketing successfully.[17]

We have suggested that local marketing will lead to increased responsibilities for the sales force and the emergence of a new trade marketing function. We believe that progressive brand managers will largely welcome rather than resist these organizational changes. Additionally, a recent survey reported that brand managers wanted to spend less time on execution-intensive marketing tasks such as sales promotion that are more susceptible to local marketing in favor of more strategic activities like advertising copy development that will contribute to the long-term health of the national brand franchise.[18]

CONCLUSION

Local marketing is a form of market segmentation. Like all segmentation schemes, it involves customizing one or more elements of the marketing program in order to achieve higher profits than would be achieved with a standardized program. However, program costs and complexity both increase. Marketers must assess whether the higher effectiveness stemming from customization (or the profit lost to more responsive competitors as a result of not customizing) more than offset the incremental costs. We believe that consumer goods and services companies will increase the proportion of their marketing expenditures assigned to local marketing programs, and that greater attention to the strategy and structure issues raised by local marketing is now necessary. The best advice in most cases will be, "Think national, act local."

Five

Dual Marketing

Many companies are dual marketers, selling the same or similar products to both individual consumers and business customers. For example, in addition to selling their products to individual consumers through dealers, automobile manufacturers sell fleets of new cars to auto rental companies, appliance manufacturers sell to builders and contractors, and food manufacturers sell through food service distributors to restaurants. Dual marketing is also widespread in the service sector. Hotels and airlines cater to both individual consumers who pay their own bills and business executives whose expenses are being covered by employers. The same person can be at different times both individual consumer and business customer.

Dual marketing is attracting increasing interest among companies that serve either the consumer or industrial market and are searching for growth opportunities. Some companies have significantly expanded in size after becoming dual marketers. Consider these examples:

- Wescon Products recently brought its precision plastic parts expertise to the consumer market with Mr. Ratchet, a line of ratchet-equipped screw socket and nut drivers.

- Efco Corp., responding to intensive price competition, began to produce commercial as well as residential windows. After several years as a dual marketer, Efco's commercial business was large enough that it could exit the residential market.[1]

- Redken Laboratories Inc. initially supplied hair care products exclusively to beauty salons and barber shops. The company started selling through retail channels after several salons were found to be repackaging Redken products for their customers to use at home.

Though dual marketing is equally relevant to industrial and consumer marketers, more industrial companies recently have expanded into consumer markets than vice versa. The reason is clear. Initially technical innovation is more likely to find an industrial application (and buyer); penetration of the consumer market follows as prices fall and user-friendly improvements are developed. The diffusion of cameras, calculators, and computers has followed this pattern. In the case of technical products, at least, it seems easier for the industrial marketer to penetrate the consumer market than vice versa. Consider, for example, IBM's success as a dual marketer of personal computers compared to Apple's problems penetrating the business market.[2]

This chapter addresses two audiences: executives at companies that are already dual marketers and those that are contemplating dual marketing. First, the benefits of dual marketing are reviewed. Many companies operating in just the industrial/institutional or consumer/retail market should consider the benefits of marketing to both sectors. Other companies that are dual marketers have managed their industrial and consumer businesses so entirely separately that the benefits of dual marketing have not been fully recognized and exploited.

The second part of the chapter reviews the challenges of dual marketing, particularly resource allocation, and offers a framework for determining how similar or different the products and programs for the two businesses should be. Finally, the organizational issues facing the dual marketer are addressed, and recommendations for coordinating the management of industrial and consumer businesses are presented.

BENEFITS OF DUAL MARKETING

If it is in an industry with dual marketing opportunities, any company that is not addressing both markets should seriously consider the benefits of doing so, especially if it is competing against dual marketers. The advantages are many.

Risk Reduction

Dual marketers reduce their risk in five ways.

(1) *Dual marketers serve a broader range of consumers* and so avoid dependency on a limited number of institutional customers. Second sources of demand are often as important as second sources of supply.

(2) *Dual marketing permits smoother production scheduling* because changes in demand in the consumer/retail market often lead or lag the industrial/institutional market. For example, the replacement market for major kitchen appliances is less vulnerable to the business cycle than the new construction market. On the other hand, retail automobile sales tend to be more vulnerable to the cycle than fleet sales.

(3) *Dual marketers can shift resources* as changing growth rates alter the relative attractiveness of the two markets. Because away-from-home food consumption continues to outpace sales growth through grocery stores, processed food manufacturers have become more interested in their food service businesses and, in some cases, in forward integration into fast-food retailing.

(4) *Dual marketers can use their production capacity more profitably* to manufacture branded products for sale in both markets. A company serving just the retail market can use its excess capacity only to manufacture private-label merchandise that may compete with and depress the price of its own branded products.

(5) *The dual marketer often has the opportunity to sell excess inventory* of a product developed for one market in the other.

Economies of Scale

The incremental volume generated by serving dual markets is especially beneficial in industries (such as automobiles and major appliances) that have a high fixed component in their cost structures. These companies attach considerable importance to maximizing capacity utilization and amortizing heavy R&D expenditures across as broad a sales base as possible.

Achieving a lower cost position through volume procurement, production, and distribution gives the dual marketer more strategic flexibility, permitting either a low cost or differentiation strategy in each market. In many product categories, from dishwashers to soft drinks, the retail and institutional markets are roughly equal in size. The closer in size they are, the greater the potential cost disadvantage of *not* being a dual marketer. Indeed, in the hotel and airline industries, the comparable size of the markets, when combined with high fixed costs, means that almost all suppliers have to be dual marketers, though they try to adapt their products to each segment (for example, through business-class seating and concierge floors).

Finally, the scale economies that dual marketers enjoy can act as a barrier to entry by foreign competition, particularly in categories such as major household appliances where offering a full product line is essential to a manufacturer's success is selling to the builder segment.

Incremental Sales

Particularly when the same products and brand names are sold in both markets, sales through institutional channels can build or reinforce consumer brand awareness and loyalty and thereby boost retail sales.

Automobile manufacturers aim to have their new models represented in auto rental fleets as soon as possible after introduction, to permit "test driving" by car rental customers and to stimulate word-of-mouth communication among consumers. In hopes of future sales, manufacturers give diaper samples to women in hospital maternity wards. A major appliance manufacturer who sells to builders of new homes hopes that, if its products perform satisfactorily, its brand will be selected by consumers when they make replacement purchases. Because most restaurants carry only one brand of ketchup and mustard, condiment manufacturers who can place their brand names in front of consumers on restaurant tables may likewise reinforce brand awareness and stimulate retail sales.

Likewise, institutional sales are often enhanced if the dual marketer's share of the retail market is strong. Most restaurants, responding to the preferences of their customers, serve Heinz ketchup rather than Hunt's or Del Monte. For the same reason, the Avis fleet includes many more General Motors cars than AMC cars. Finally, many builders believe that consumers treat well-known brand names on kitchen appliances as indicators of the overall quality of new houses.

If a brand's presence in one market declines, its sales in the other market may be adversely affected. As more restaurants make pots of decaffeinated coffee, the visibility of Sanka packets has declined and the brand's retail sales have stabilized.

Advertising Credibility

A strong presence in the institutional market can lend credibility to the product in the minds of individual consumers. Consumers may be impressed if advertising states that:

- An over-the-counter pharmaceutical is often prescribed by doctors or used in hospitals;

- A particular personal computer is the brand most often selected by *Fortune* 500 companies;

- A brand of coffee is served in some of the nation's finest restaurants; or

- A brand of carpet cleaner is also widely used in office buildings.

Such advertising, often backed up by endorsements from institutional customers, may enhance the perceived value of these products among consumers and reduce the perceived risk.

New Product Development

The dual marketer has an opportunity to achieve economies by applying the results of research and development efforts in both industrial/institutional and consumer/retail markets. More dollars can therefore be committed to research and development activity than would otherwise be the case.

Often, however, new products are developed with one market in mind and are later adapted for launch in the second market. Many products developed for the fast-food service industry—frozen pizza, boneless ribs, and fruit syrup concentrates, for example—have later been introduced successfully in the retail channel.[3] And because restaurants are more sensitive than individual consumers to storage costs, many processing and packaging innovations—such as UHT technology, aseptic packaging, and modified atmosphere storage—were first developed in response to their needs.

Such "technology transfer" can also work in the other direction. Shasta decided to offer its sodas to the retail market in a unique eight-ounce package size but found more enthusiasm for the new packaging in the hospital segment of the institutional market. Patients could handle the eight-ounce package more easily than the traditional sixteen-ounce size, and product waste was greatly reduced.

Test Marketing

Most consumer-directed programs rely more on pull marketing than their industrial counterparts, which tend to emphasize push marketing. In the case of low-fixed-cost products, where scale economies are not critical, it is sometimes practical to introduce a new product first in the industrial market, where marketing launch costs are lower. Customer reaction can be tested and any necessary product modifications made before investing the pull marketing dollars required for a retail market introduction. For example, to test consumer reactions, Ford installed airbags in 20% of the Tempos used by Travelers Insurance salespeople.

An initial launch in the institutional market can build consumer and trade awareness, thus lowering the marketing cost of the subsequent retail launch. McCain's Foods, a major force in the Canadian food service industry, traditionally has built initial volume for its new products in the food service sector, using the profits to finance subsequent product launches in the consumer market.

Sometimes, however, a successful product launch in the retail market is necessary to attract the attention of more cautious institutional customers. The success of G.D. Searle Co.'s Equal sugar substitute in the retail market boosted the interest of manufacturers of carbonated beverages and other products in using NutraSweet (aspartame) as a sugar substitute in their products. In turn, inclusion of the NutraSweet name on their products' packages reinforced Equal's retail sales.[4] Similarly, Chemical Bank is now finding it easier to sell licenses of its Pronto home banking software to other banks around the country because of its success in launching the Pronto system with its own retail customers in New York.

Customer Reach

Institutional purchasers typically buy in larger quantities than do individual consumers. Often, however, there are small institutional purchasers who cannot be served efficiently by an institutional marketing organization, particularly one using an account management system. In the absence of a retail marketing effort, sales to these customers might be lost. But the dual marketer gives these small institutional purchasers the opportunity to buy and perhaps negotiate a quantity discount through the retail channel.

For example, an increasing number of small businesses are involved in home lawn care. As a result, Toro Company distributors sell some commercial-grade lawn mowers through consumer rather than commercial dealers in order to reach this segment. Likewise, small businesses often buy personal computers through retail computer stores and small builders sometimes use retail hardware centers rather than builder supply houses. When the retail channel also serves part of the institutional market, as in these cases, a manufacturer is likely to enhance its influence with the retail channel if it serves both markets.

Market Intelligence

Market intelligence is often a major objective of the company that becomes a dual marketer for defensive reasons. The dual marketer receives three market intelligence benefits:

(1) When institutional and retail markets overlap, the dual marketer enjoys more complete information about the size of the institutional market.

(2) If the rate of product use is faster in one market than the other, the dual marketer is apprised of potential problems. Automobile manufacturers monitor the incidence of technical and service problems in the new models they sell to auto rental companies. In that way they are prepared to respond when the same problems

show up later in the less heavily driven models of individual consumers.

(3) The dual marketer can monitor competitive activity and new product development more thoroughly and is, therefore, less likely to be taken by surprise by a competitor than the focused marketer. For example, Chesebrough-Pond's Vaseline brand dominated the retail petroleum jelly market but was poorly represented in the hospital market. Johnson & Johnson identified the need for a soluble jelly in hospitals and introduced K-Y Jelly in that market, using the profits from hospital sales to fund the product's launch in the retail market. If the Vaseline brand had been sold aggressively in the hospital market, Johnson & Johnson might not have been permitted to establish a beachhead from which to attack the larger and more lucrative retail market.

Shared Marketing Techniques

Consumer marketers can learn tools and approaches from institutional marketers, and vice versa. Account management, long practiced by commercial banks for their larger customers, is increasingly being used by consumer marketers to provide services tailored to their principal retail accounts. Likewise, the pull marketing techniques commonly used to reach individual consumers are increasingly being applied by institutional marketers. For example, the food service division of Campbell Soup Company has announced a consumer advertising campaign jointly funded with Burger King to promote a new line of branded soups available through Burger King restaurants.

Because more food service distributors are developing their own private label products, food manufacturers are increasingly interested in developing pull programs that reach restaurant operators directly. Hence, Nabisco's recent introductory marketing program for Royal Choice Tea in the food service market bore all the trademarks of a consumer marketer's branding, packaging, and communications thinking.

SAME PRODUCTS, DIFFERENT PROGRAMS?

Of course, dual marketing poses challenges as well as benefits. In becoming a dual marketer, a company risks eroding its distinctive competence, diluting management effort and focus, increasing organizational complexity, and being perceived as trying to be all things to all markets.

Problems in Resource Allocation and Product Standardization

Resource allocation problems become more frequent, particularly when a product common to the two businesses is in short supply and must be allocated, or when the smaller of the two businesses offers greater long-term profit potential and therefore commands relatively more resources than its share of current sales would suggest. Two examples:

- G.D. Searle has separate business units selling NutraSweet to industrial customers and Equal brand sweetener through retail channels. A temporary shortage of aspartame relative to demand meant that development of the Equal retail brand had to be slowed to enable Searle to meet its commitments to its industrial customers.

- In 1985, Apple Computer withdrew its Lisa model from retail distribution and announced a concentrated effort to penetrate the business market. Apple dealers protested that the company was diverting resources from the retail to the business market and called for a more balanced approach.[5]

The more standardized the products and programs targeting the two markets, the fewer the problems of resource allocation. The benefits the dual marketer enjoys—particularly scale economies—are greater when products and programs directed at the two markets are more alike than unlike. The dual marketer has to determine:

- The degree to which products and programs should be standardized for the two markets. To arrive at this decision, management must calculate the cost and revenue implications of different levels of standardization.

- The appropriate degree of organizational integration and coordination, given the level of product and program standardization. Specifically, should the two businesses have common management in either planning, R&D, manufacturing, and/or marketing?

On the first issue, the dual marketer can choose from among the four options represented in Figure 5.1. Option 1 maximizes scale economies but leaves the dual marketer vulnerable to focused marketers who tailor products and programs to either the retail or institutional market. Option 4 leaves the dual marketer exposed to a producer following Option 1 who may be able, through scale economies, to achieve unit prices so much lower than those of focused competitors that many consumers will be willing to trade off some degree of market tailoring for the level of savings offered. Option 2 is frequently followed by companies for which the principal scale economies are achieved in production, not marketing. In such cases, different "optional" features and brand names may be attached to the same core product in order to tailor the total offering to each market.

	Same Programs	Different Programs
Same Products	1	2
Different Products	3	4

Figure 5.1. The Dual Marketer's Options.

Adaptation through Different Products

Despite the opportunities for adaptation through program rather than product tailoring, many dual marketers continue to target substantially different products at the retail and institutional markets. Different products (Options 3 and 4) are more likely to be sold when:

(1) *The relative importance of product benefits and the decision-making process is different for end users of the product in the two markets.* The business executive entitled to a company car is not at all price-sensitive compared to the individual consumer. If anything, the executive is sensitive to how high rather than how low the price is. Similarly, when the consumer at the end of the institutional channel purchases the product as part of a larger package, she or he may also be less price-sensitive than the retail buyer. For example, when it comes to kitchen appliances, the new-home buyer is typically more concerned with their quality than their price because their cost is such a small percentage of the total price of the house.

On the other hand, when the purchaser and user are one and the same in both retail and institutional markets—as in the case of a consumer buying ice cream at a fountain outlet and in a supermarket—the marketing program is more readily standardized.

(2) *The relative importance of product benefits is different for intermediaries in the two channels.* For example, both supermarkets and restaurants are interested in efficient packaging that minimizes their handling and storage costs. Restaurants, however, may prefer individual portion packaging that is convenient and limits opportunities for employee abuse through yield extension. In addition, the packaging of products sold to restaurants must be more robust if the product is to stay wholesome under potentially poor storage conditions.

(3) *The end user in the institutional market receives the product in a different form from the retail purchaser*. Restaurant patrons often receive tea in a bag with a brand nametag attached, but coffee is usually poured from a pot. Consistency between the retail and the institutional product is more important in the first case than the second.

(4) *Different channels are used to reach the two markets*. This is much more the case with personal computers than with automobiles. General Motors makes the same car models for both institutional and retail markets and therefore can distribute all its cars, including fleet sales, through the same GM-authorized dealers.

(5) *Different competitors are important in each market*, and these competitors manufacture, at competitive prices, products finely tailored to the needs of their respective customers.

(6) *Scale economies are insignificant* beyond a production volume lower than that necessary to serve the company's customers in the smaller of the two markets.

Tailoring the Marketing Mix

As shown in Figure 5.2, the dual marketer has the opportunity to tailor not only the product but also each element of the marketing mix to the needs of the retail and institutional markets. Three points should be noted:

- *First*, the pressure for differentiation is greater and the cost penalty in lost scale economies lower as one moves down the list.

- *Second*, some mix elements can be standardized more easily than others. Advertising, for example, is more controllable by the marketer than the choice of distribution channels.

- *Third*, the standardization decision on each mix element is not independent. For example, it makes no sense for prices to be

	Same	Different
Product Features		
Brand Name		
Pricing		
Product Positioning		
Advertising		
Packaging		
Distribution Channels		
Sales Force		
Sales Promotion		

Figure 5.2. Marketing Program Planning Grid for Dual Marketers.

different if other program elements are the same. The mixes for both markets must be integrated and internally consistent.

Whether a dual marketer's products and programs are similar or different, problems can arise, opportunities can be lost, and strategic conflicts can occur if there is insufficient coordination between the marketing mix used by the consumer/retail business and the industrial/institutional business. Following are four examples.

PRODUCT DIVERSION.   A company selling the same line of fertilizers to retail and institutional customers was forced into a price war by a competitor in the institutional market. It soon became more attractive for lawn and garden distributors to purchase the products from the company's institutional customers than from the company itself. Similarly, 3M found that weak retail sales of its Post-It notes were due in part to office workers taking supplies for home use. 3M has since developed Post-It line extensions in different colors and sizes for the retail market. To avoid product diversion problems, some companies sell the same products with different brand names to the two markets. In so doing, however, they forfeit some of the communications impact advantages available to the dual marketer.

PRICING.   The consumer sales manager of a leading British automobile manufacturer wanted to focus the advertising for a particular model on a price comparison with its closest competitors. The manager of fleet sales objected, arguing that image was more important to corporate executives who increasingly choose their cars from lists preapproved by their companies. He argued that a price-oriented advertising campaign targeted at the retail consumer would reduce his sales.

SCHEDULING.   An innovative adhesive applicator was developed by corporate R&D at the request of the consumer products division of a major adhesive manufacturer. The industrial products group was permitted to incorporate the applicator into a new product of its own, though it was understood that the consumer products division would do the initial launch. Competitive problems delayed the consumer launch. When the industrial group went on with its schedule, the consumer group complained that its thunder had been stolen.

EXCLUSIVITY.   In the interests of efficiency, a home furnishings manufacturer decided to standardize its product line, making the same patterns available to both retail stores and professional decorators. The firm's share of the professional decorator market dropped significantly because competitive firms continued to offer them exclusive patterns. As a result, the company reversed its decision.

In trying to determine the appropriate degree of product and program standardization, dual marketers often find it useful to distinguish between *cost*-related mix elements (such as product design) and *demand*-related elements (such as brand name and advertising). As Figure 5.3 shows, standardization realizes both production and communications economies, but at the expense of a focused approach for each market. The dual marketer must weigh the cost of tailoring against the additional sales and profits that may be realized.

		Demand-Related Marketing Mix Elements	
		Two Markets Independent	Two Markets Dependent
Cost-Related Marketing Mix Elements	Two Markets Independent	No Economies (Adaptation)	Communication Economies
	Two Markets Dependent	Production Economies	Full Economies (Standardization)

Figure 5.3. Economies of Standardization for Dual Marketers.

INTEGRATION OR INSULATION?

As the preceding examples clearly indicate, dual marketers must closely coordinate their retail and institutional businesses. Yet, despite increasing recognition of the similarities between industrial and consumer marketing,[6] most dual marketers have traditionally managed each business through a separate organization. Despite higher administrative overheads, this approach ensures that the smaller of the two businesses receives focused managerial attention. However, the result has often been to insulate one business from the other, and to risk failing to exploit fully the potential advantages of closer coordination. It must be emphasized that the benefits of being a dual marketer are realized only if the two businesses are coordinated.

Of course, coordination can have many meanings. For the dual marketer who targets different products and programs at the institutional and retail markets, coordination may mean merely that the functional managers of two separate businesses share information. For the dual marketer who targets the same products and programs at both markets, coordination may extend to full organizational integration across all functions, as depicted in the left-hand column of Figure 5.4.

Many companies quite appropriately use a hybrid approach dictated in part by the size of their industrial and consumer businesses. General Electric Co.'s Lamp Products Division used to manage these two businesses through a common functional organization. By 1970, the businesses had become large enough to justify a separate sales force for each. By 1982, a general manager was running each business as a separate division. Coordination, however, continues to be close because each division makes some products that are sold in both markets.

Whatever approach is taken, top management should heed the following recommendations to ensure that:

- The two businesses complement rather than compromise each other's efforts; and

Functions	Handle Two Businesses with	
	Same Organization	Separate Organizations
Strategic Planning		
Research and Development		
Procurement		
Manufacturing		
Marketing		
Selling		
	Integration	Insulation

Figure 5.4. Organization Planning for the Dual Marketer.

- The advantages and limitations of greater coordination are constantly being evaluated.

ENSURE EQUAL STATUS.   Inevitably, the status and morale of executives in a dual marketer's retail and institutional businesses will depend in part upon the relative importance of each to the company's overall sales and profits. However, in too many companies that manage the two businesses through separate organizations, the consumer marketers view themselves as superior in skills and importance to their counterparts in the institutional business. For example, the food service divisions of major grocery products manufacturers often have been viewed as second-rate marketers whose sales merely absorb excess capacity rather than as important sources of new product ideas. Top management must work to develop mutual respect, cooperation, and a perception of equal status between the retail and institutional executives.

ENCOURAGE EXECUTIVE EXCHANGE.   Because marketing skills developed for the retail business may be applicable to the institutional business, and vice versa, management should consider developing career paths that move executives from one business to the other. Such movement is easier, of course, if organization structures are similar in both businesses. Grocery products manufacturers, for example, typically use a product management structure for both their consumer marketing and food service businesses. Others, however, use product managers to run their retail businesses but market managers to run their institutional businesses, first, because institutional customers often want to purchase a full line of products and, second, because market segments of institutional customers differ in their product mix needs. In these cases, career paths can be established to permit an institutional market manager to be transferred to a product management position in the consumer business, or vice versa.

COORDINATE STRATEGIC PLANNING. Even if the retail and institutional businesses are managed through separate organizations, top management should conduct strategic planning for both in tandem. It is necessary to understand their comparative sales and profit potential and competitive vulnerabilities to decide the appropriate strategic roles of each business and the appropriate allocation of marketing, manufacturing, and research and development resources. In the absence of joint strategic planning, disputes are more likely to occur over which business should have priority in the allocation of resources.

COORDINATE MANUFACTURING. The company's strategic plans should provide guidance on which business should have priority and which customers should be put on allocation in the event capacity is fully utilized, and which should receive higher quality raw materials in the event of variability. Such coordination is more likely to be needed if, in response to scale economies, the retail and institutional products are designed so that the same production lines are used for both.

COORDINATE R&D. Some companies with separate marketing organizations for their retail and institutional businesses also have separate R&D organizations, especially when the relative importance of customer benefits in the two markets varies substantially or when adoption of new products in one market typically leads the other market by several years. The challenge in such cases is:

- *First*, to ensure that technology is not developed for one market without considering how it will then be applied to the other, and

- *Second*, to achieve efficient technology transfer so that R&D efforts for one part of the business can be quickly exploited by the other.

Joint new product planning committees, which include R&D and marketing representatives from both businesses, are valuable for this purpose. At Black & Decker, the technology for the housewares division's highly successful Spotliter and Dustbuster products was transferred in this way from the outdoor and power tool division.

Another way to facilitate technology transfer is to have R&D specialists who cover particular products for both the institutional and the retail markets. This approach is used by companies such as Rubbermaid and Land O Lakes. For example, the technology developed by Land O Lakes to make Scram Blend, a scrambled egg mixture for food service, was quickly adapted to make a new consumer product, Pour-A-Quiche.

Opportunistic adaptation can be encouraged if the business that adopts a technology or product is not required to pay fees or royalties to the business that developed it. Such transfer payments are less likely to become an issue if a single R&D resource serves both businesses.

COORDINATE PRODUCT MARKETING. If separate marketing organizations handle the two parts of the business, it is essential to have communication and agreement on:

- Whether a new product should be launched at the same time in both markets or, if not—given potential profits, competitive pressures, the pace of technology change, and the transferability of success from one market to the other—in which market the product should be introduced first;

- How rapidly product demand should be developed and the projected life cycle of the product in each market; and

- To what degree product features and marketing programs—

especially pricing and communications—can and should be standardized.

CONCLUSION

Dual marketing represents both an opportunity and a challenge. A three-part process is recommended for executives who are contemplating selling their products to both consumers and the industrial market:

(1) Evaluate the benefits of being a dual marketer in your business.

(2) Determine the appropriate degree of standardization or differentiation in the products and programs directed at the two markets.

(3) Integrate the functional management of the two businesses where appropriate and ensure a high degree of coordination.

Many companies are already dual marketers, but few yet manage to maximum advantage the opportunities provided by being in both businesses.

Six

——

Licensing

The licensing of technology has long been familiar to industrial marketers as a means of accelerating the pace of market development and funding research. Licensing has traditionally been less widespread in consumer markets, with the exception of Coca-Cola and other beverage makers that license bottlers to produce and sell their brands.

What proprietary technology is to the industrial marketer, however, brand franchises and logos are to the consumer marketer. The most common licensing agreements on consumer goods are those permitting licensees to use names, logos, and characters owned by others on products they make. For instance:

- Questor Corporation owns the Spalding name. Of the Spalding products made in 1980, Questor made nearly all—and lost $12.6 million on sales of $273 million. By 1983, licensees were making all Spalding products; Questor earned $12 million on sales of $250 million.

- Pierre Cardin has issued more than 500 licenses and Yves St. Laurent more than 200 to companies that use their logos on goods manufactured to their specifications. Sports and rock stars also authorize manufacture of apparel and other products carrying their names.

- Product licensing of cartoon and fantasy characters, such as E.T., are proving so lucrative that some companies are even designing characters like Strawberry Shortcake for the express purpose of licensing them. Sales of products carrying the Strawberry Short-cake name, licensed by American Greetings Corporation, exceeded $100 million in 1983.

- Sales of licensed products have quadrupled from $6.5 billion in 1978 to $26.7 billion in 1983. No consumer marketer should consider its business or product category immune to inroads from licensed products. Consider these two examples:

  Binney & Smith dominated the $5 million children's putty market with Silly Putty until several small businesses entered the market with licensed products such as Bugs Bunny Putty and Spiderman Putty. Despite rolling back wholesale prices 25%, Silly Putty lost ten share points in three years.

  A large mattress manufacturer, Englander Company, was forced into bankruptcy by a price war initiated by a Sealy licensee, Ohio Mattress Company. After becoming one of the industry's lowest cost producers, Ohio Mattress began shipping products to retailers in the market areas of other Sealy licensees for as little as two-thirds of their regular prices. The result was a nationwide price war.

What factors account for the surge of interest? First, media cost inflation and advertising clutter have raised the price of establishing a brand name. Shortening product life cycles in many categories also have made marketing investments riskier. Moreover, consumers, besieged by brand name overload, are looking for ways to simplify their decision-making processes across categories. Finally, some marketers claim, almost all the best brand names have already been registered by one company or another.

To consumer marketers these factors suggest that they should develop and launch only brands with the potential to straddle several product categories. The situation further suggests that they should scrutinize opportunities for extending existing brand franchises. This step can enhance the cost efficiency of advertising, heighten consumer awareness, permit billboarding of packages at the point-of-purchase, stimulate trade interest in promoting the brand, and encourage consumers to try products carrying the familiar name.

Companies can extend brand franchises in two ways. They can finance and carry out the effort themselves or—at less risk and perhaps no less potential return—grant to others the right to do so.

WHY LICENSE?

There are almost as many objectives for licensing as there are licensing agreements. Following are the most important reasons to license.

LAUNCH A NATIONAL BRAND. Licensing agreements are especially advantageous in this respect for smaller manufacturers aiming to add to their profit margins. BASF Wyandotte, a producer of private-label antifreeze, wanted to launch a brand nationally to compete against Union Carbide's Prestone. But BASF estimated the cost of developing national brand recognition and distribution at $15 million annually for ten years. Meanwhile, STP was interested in marketing an antifreeze carrying its well-known name, but the company lacked production capacity and expertise. A licensing agreement was struck—the STP name on a BASF-manufactured antifreeze.

A second example illustrates the same point. Chipman-Union, Inc., a private-label manufacturer of men's hosiery, licensed the use of the Odor-Eaters name from Combe, Inc. for a new line of premium high-margin, deodorizing athletic socks. Chipman-Union hopes eventually to use profits from this venture to launch its own brand.

QUICKLY PENETRATE NEW MARKETS. Cross-licensing agreements have long been common among pharmaceutical concerns that have sales and distribution strengths only in particular geographic areas but have developed products with worldwide market potential. Like other beverage manufacturers, Löwenbräu has used licensing agreements to boost its worldwide sales rapidly without committing capital to build bottling plants. Löwenbräu, far from being the market share leader in West Germany, looks to profits from offshore licensing to generate the funds needed for greater market penetration at home.

SHARE THE INVESTMENT RISKS. In no two consumer goods markets are demand patterns more unpredictable, life cycles shorter, and industry fragmentation more evident than in the toy and fashion industries. Since many toy manufacturers cannot risk big investments in promoting new products of their own, they are increasingly licensing characters and concepts and trying to build consumer awareness of them through movies, cartoons, comic books, or greeting cards. As indicated earlier, the entertainment industry and greeting card companies now dream up characters with lifestyles appealing to specific target groups—solely to license their use.

Like the toy makers, apparel manufacturers are "selling" the use of designer names and sharing the cost of building consumer awareness with licensees. For the latter, the perceived differentiation and consequent price premium that designer labels can command often more than compensate for royalty payments.

ADD TO NAME AWARENESS. Faced with legal restrictions on advertising, tobacco and liquor manufacturers continually search for new communication vehicles to reach their targets. R.J. Reynolds Tobacco Company and Philip Morris, Inc. now license leisure apparel carrying respectively the Camel and Marlboro names. (In both cases the advertising focuses on lifestyles and consumer ego needs.)

To reinforce brand awareness via licensing of related products, Sunkist Growers, Inc. gave General Cinema Corporation the right to sell Sunkist orange soda. Doubtless, Sunkist recognized that the teenage movie audiences of today, as the homemakers of tomorrow, will eventually be buying oranges in supermarkets.

MAXIMIZE EXISTING LINES' PROFITABILITY.   Many food companies, facing a future of lower population and sales growth, are looking for ways to enhance revenues from their existing brands. They are seeking to license the use of corporate characters (such as Ernie Keebler and the Campbell Kids) or brand characters (such as Kellogg Company's Tony the Tiger and Nabisco Brands' Mr. Peanut) to makers of children's products. These arrangements are designed not only to yield royalties but also to enhance sales of the food products, since more and more children's toys and apparel are appearing in the aisles of supermarkets as stores add more high-margin general merchandise.

Nonfood companies such as Greyhound are also exploring opportunities to license well-recognized names and logos. The Greyhound logo might be especially marketable since the company's buses act as moving billboards, forever reinforcing consumer name awareness.

REVIVE MATURE BRANDS.   Such brands often contribute too little a percentage of total sales to earn much management attention. An alternative to selling them is to license the right to make and market them to a license having enough expertise and a strong commitment. In 1981, for example, Purex Corporation licensed Jeffrey Martin, Inc. to market Doan's pills and Ayds. Through Jeffrey Martin's aggressive advertising, sales of these products have grown considerably.

CONTROL SUBSIDIARIES' POLICIES.   Nestlé requires its 75 operating subsidiaries around the world to register in Switzerland all brands they sell locally and to pay headquarters at Vevey nominal royalties for their use. This procedure enables Nestlé to exercise subtle control over its subsidiaries' product policy and to standardize the presentation of company and brand names and logos worldwide.

KEEP A CONSUMER FRANCHISE.   When it acquired General Electric's small appliance division, Black & Decker obtained the right to use the

G.E. name for three years. This move has given Black & Decker the time to develop its trade relationships and gradually phase in products carrying its own name.

COMMON PROBLEMS

When licensing agreements fail to live up to expectations, the cause is often overlicensing or undercommitment. The former occurs when too many licensees are recruited too fast. Quality control becomes harder and the licenser risks debasement of the brand name, thus shortening the useful life and revenue potential of the brand, opening the door to competitors, and straining the loyalties of licensees.

Izod Lacoste ran into these problems when it licensed use of its alligator logo on a wide variety of clothing and accessories, including wallets and even sunglasses. Some licensees failed to meet quality standards, so the General Mills subsidiary had to bring lawsuits against them. More important, Izod's image of exclusivity and its licensees' ability to command premium prices for Izod products faded in favor of Ralph Lauren's Polo logo. Izod earnings fell 25% in fiscal 1984. Last January General Mills announced it was putting Izod and other nonfood operations up for sale.

Partly as a result of such experiences, many retailers have become cautious about stocking up on licensed apparel, particularly merchandise carrying the names of rock stars whose popularity can wilt rapidly.

A second source of problems is undercommitment, actual or perceived. This can arise when the licensee or licenser enters an agreement for defensive reasons. Licensees may sign agreements to preempt competitors or to secure information without seriously intending to exploit their rights for profit. Chemical Bank has been trying to license its Pronto home banking software to other U.S. banks. But those institutions most interested in home banking are developing their own software independently or jointly. Many Pronto licensees, cautious while waiting to see how the technology develops, therefore will probably be slower than Chemical would wish in offering home banking to consumers.

If a licenser suspects that prospective licensees may be defensively motivated, it should not grant exclusive market rights. If the licenser does, it cannot threaten to or actually license a competitor in the initial licensee's market.

Likewise, licensers sometimes sign agreements without a sense of deep commitment. For example, when a company has to license a competitor because trade customers insist on the availability of at least two competing supply sources, the licensee will usually receive weak support from its reluctant licenser.

In addition, potential licensees should be wary of acquiring rights to the use of names whose owners appear to have no serious interest. Sometimes, after negotiating a series of agreements, a company will reduce its marketing support for a name in the hope that the advertising to which its licensees have committed themselves in their contracts will sustain consumer awareness. A stipulation in the contracts calling for the name owner's marketing support will help avoid that situation. When characters rather than brand names are licensed, however, such guarantees are hard to come by because of the unpredictability of movie and television audiences. Poor results may cause a withdrawal of the movie or show in which the licensed character appears.

A further risk some licensees face is dependence on sales of licensed products at the expense of goods bearing their own company or brand names, whose marketing and longevity are far more under their control. Miles Laboratories phased out its Chocks brand of chewable children's vitamins in favor of the licensed Flintstones line; financial performance improved but at the price of some loss in marketing control. Licensed items now account for more than half of toy sales as manufacturers have bowed to the notion that children dominate toy-buying decisions, and they look for characters rather than brand names at the point-of-purchase. In an effort to retain control of their businesses, some toy makers are developing their own characters and licensing their use to the media.

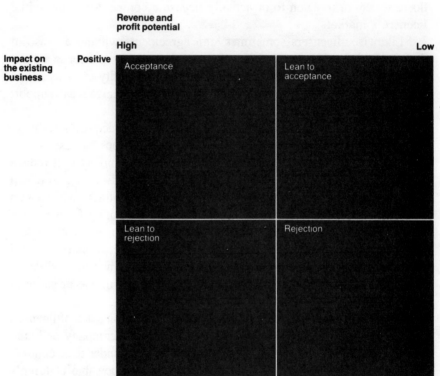

Figure 6.1. Opportunity Evaluation Matrix.

EFFECTIVE ARRANGEMENTS

Following are six recommendations to licensers to guide the development and implementation of agreements. The same advice is relevant to licensees.

(1) *Develop a strategy.* Too many companies view royalty payments, which generally run from 6% to 10% of product sales, merely as windfall revenues. So they devote insufficient time to developing a licensing strategy and managing the agreement. Before sitting down to negotiate, ask yourself the following questions:

What percentage of total revenues do we want to get from this?

What is the market potential for licensing names in our product categories?

Should we seek out partners or merely respond to approaches made to us?

What criteria should we establish to screen prospects?

What restrictions and incentives should we write into our agreements?

Ideally, what do we want each party to give and to receive in any arrangement?

(2) *Evaluate alternatives.* Your two key criteria for evaluating opportunities should be (a) revenue and earnings potential and (b) impact on the sales of other products carrying the same name. (See Figure 6.1.)

(3) *Do consumer research.* To assess those opportunities you must first understand consumer and trade attitudes—positive and negative—toward your company or brand names. Survey research can yield an indication of the credibility of extending your names to other product categories, and can guide the development of standardized names and logo graphics to maximize impact at the point-of-purchase. The Weight Watchers organization, which started as a chain of diet clinics, has extended its name to a variety of low-calorie food products. But the impact has not been maximized, partly because the presentation of the name and logo is not coordinated among Weight Watchers licensees.

(4) *Protect your property*. Establish quality standards governing licensees' manufacturing and marketing efforts. Be patient and select only those partners able to meet your quality standards. Be prepared to police them by taking periodic product samples and making unexpected plant visits.

But be a coach as well as a policeman: help the licensee do a high-quality job in marketing as well as manufacturing. Löwenbräu not only requires its licensees around the world to send product samples each month to its Munich laboratories for testing; the company also lends its licensees technicians to help them solve production problems. In addition to following these practices, Spalding often sends its marketing executives with licensee salespeople into the field to make calls on store buyers.

(5) *Maintain product leadership*. The surest way to maintain the loyalty of your licensees and the value of your company or brand name is through product superiority and technical leadership. Although Spalding does no manufacturing, it has a large staff of sporting goods designers. Design leadership has helped the company win endorsements such as the National Basketball Association contract, which Wilson Sporting Goods held for 37 years. Such endorsements further reinforce the strength of the company or brand name and licensee loyalty.

(6) *Share risks and rewards*. The healthiest licensing agreement is one in which the licensed product has equal strategic importance and potential profits for both licensee and licenser. You may find it worthwhile to make a trade with the licensee: a percentage point on the royalty rate for a commitment to higher quality standards or a greater marketing effort. Be sure you understand the prospective partner's cost structure, and be prepared to share your marketing plans so that the licensee can fairly assess your estimates of the likely sales and income.

Finally, discuss how each party can verify that the other is fulfilling its commitments and how disagreements will be dealt with. A mutually rewarding, sustainable licensing agreement requires careful relationship management, and that must begin at the negotiating table.

Seven

Nonstore Marketing

Will nonstore marketing, sometimes called direct marketing, become the next revolution in retailing? According to several optimistic forecasts, the answer is an unquestionable yes. There is already in place a variety of established selling techniques that permit consumers to purchase products and services without having to visit retail stores, and several new approaches have been made possible by recent technological advances. (See Table 7.1.)

It is, however, far easier to describe the various types of nonstore marketing than to distinguish it as a whole from other forms of retailing, for the line between in-store and nonstore marketing is fuzzy. Consider, for example, that:

- A consumer may become confident enough to purchase merchandise by mail order only after having shopped at a store several times. Alternatively, a catalog may interest a consumer in a product that he or she subsequently purchases in a store.

Table 7.1. TYPES OF NONSTORE MARKETING*

ESTABLISHED METHODS

Mail-order catalogs

General merchandisers (Sears and J.C. Penney), department stores (Bloomingdale's and Macy's), catalog showrooms (Best Products and Service Merchandise), and specialty merchandisers (L.L. Bean and Horchow) periodically mail catalogs to targeted groups of current and potential customers. Consumers may respond either by placing a telephone or mail order or, more traditionally, by visiting a retail outlet or a catalog showroom to make an in-store purchase.

Direct response advertising

Consumers become aware of a product through print or broadcast advertising or through a telephone call from a salesperson and may purchase the product by agreeing to the salesperson's offer, by making a telephone call (usually to a toll-free number), or by returning an order form through the mail. Frequently, direct response merchandisers who use broadcast advertising pay the station a commission for each inquiry or order received in lieu of paying for advertising time.

Home selling

Consumers learn about a product in a face-to-face meeting with the seller's agent. Fuller Brush and Avon, for example, use door-to-door salespeople; Stanley Home Products and Tupperware use party plan selling; and Amway uses a legal "pyramid" selling approach. Although home selling is an expensive way of delivering product information to consumers, it does allow for product demonstration, personal service, and immediate delivery.

Vending machines

These machines, which represent a mixture of in-store and nonstore marketing, enable manufacturers and wholesalers to increase the intensity of retail distribution and, by extension, the convenience of such buy-on-impulse items as candy, beverages, and cigarettes. These purchases add up: throughout the United States, consumers drop some 200,000 coins every minute into six million vending machines.†

Table 7.1.   (Cont.)

NEW TECHNOLOGIES

Interactive cable television
An interactive cable system like the Warner-Amex Cable Communications QUBE service in Columbus, Ohio, permits viewers to purchase merchandise displayed on their television screens and charge the cost to a credit card or bank account by punching a keypad. The system offers viewers the convenience of making impulse purchases from an armchair, without the need for even a telephone call.

Interactive information retrieval
Systems like Canada's Telidon, Britain's Prestel, and France's Antiope permit customers to use a computer data bank by telephone or by a two-way cable system. The desired information appears on the home television screen, which is connected to the telephone system through a decoder. By operating a keypad device, a consumer can control the information appearing on the screen. Viewdata Corporation of America, a subsidiary of the Knight-Ridder newspaper chain, is currently testing such a system in Coral Gables, Florida.

Videocassettes and videodiscs
These devices, which have to date been sold principally as a means of enabling consumers to record television programs that they would otherwise miss, are thought by some to have significant promise as advertising media. According to direct marketing expert Maxwell Sroge, "Discalogs [videodisc catalogs] will be in the mail within the next three years."‡

---

*A detailed typology of nonstore retailing approaches is included in William Davidson and Alice Rodgers, "Nonstore Retailing: Its Importance to and Impact on Merchandise Suppliers and Competitive Channels," Management Horizons Inc. working paper, Columbus, Ohio, 1977.
†"Vending Unit Sales Slide with Economy," *New York Times*, August 8, 1980.
‡Quoted in "Home Video Part 2: What's Its Future as an Ad Medium?" *Marketing and Media Decisions*, March 1980, p. 104.

- Every year, department and specialty stores with annual sales of $75 million or more generally issue 6 to 20 catalogs with a circulation of from 100,000 to a million each. Among typical department stores, telephone and mail-generated orders account for 15% of total volume during the Christmas season,[1] and old-line retailers such as Sears and Lazarus are experimenting with interactive cable television to sell their products and services.

- Mail-order houses like Talbots and Carroll Reed are expanding their retail store networks. As of this writing, Talbots has 16 stores and Carroll Reed, 15 (excluding ski shops).

- Manufacturers that traditionally sold their products only through retail outlets are adding direct marketing as an additional mode of distribution. Nearly 50 companies in the *Fortune* 500 have already become members of the Direct Mail/Marketing Association.[2]

- Fruit growers, cattle breeders, and cheese producers are discovering the fast-growing mail-order food business. Consumers can now buy "gourmet" foods from some 500 mail-order food houses, which do three-quarters of their annual volume during the Christmas season.[3] Conglomerates like Tenneco (House of Almonds), Greyhound (Pfaelzer Brothers steaks), and Metromedia (Figi's cheese) have already entered this high-margin specialty business.

These developments, among others, lead us to agree with the optimistic forecasters that the growth of nonstore marketing in recent years has been impressive and that its promise remains bright. At the same time, however, we do foresee several limits to its unrestrained growth in the future and are, therefore, not convinced that it will soon revolutionize retailing.

MARKETING FAILURE—AND SUCCESS

Established forms of direct marketing produced mixed results during the 1970s. To understand clearly their future potential, we need to examine the reasons for their past failures and successes.

Grocery Shopping

During the past 10 years, several attempts have been made to automate nonstore grocery shopping. One of the first was launched in San Diego by Telemart Enterprises, Inc. in the fall of 1970. In two weeks of operation, Telemart received some 23,000 orders (with no minimum amount required) and had to close its doors. The warehouse employees who collected ordered items and put them into shopping bags simply could not keep pace: they were able to fill less than one-fifth of the orders. Telemart even resorted to shutting off the telephones, but too late.

According to *Computerworld*, the Telemart system worked like this: "A shopper would call in and give his or her credit number. The order taker would interconnect the shopper with a 'talking computer' for a three-way conversation. Using a catalog, the shopper would list the desired items. The computer would record the items ordered, verify that they were in stock, give a verbal response on the price of each item, provide totals, and mention any specials of the day.

"The computer would then print out an optimized collection list for the central distribution center, select the most efficient truck routing for delivery of goods to the customer, maintain all records of accounts payable and receivable, and keep a running tabulation of inventories."[4]

Store-to-Door, a system similar to Telemart's, opened two years later in Sacramento and lasted a little longer—from September 7 to November 4, 1972. In this case, the computer, not overacceptance, was to blame. The system was supposed to handle 3,400 orders a day but actually was able to handle only 500. Although Store-to-Door had promised afternoon delivery on items ordered in the morning and next-morning delivery on items ordered in the afternoon, its delivery times quickly began to slip as a result of delays in computerized order processing and invoice printing.

The next entrant into the field was Call-a-Mart in Louisville, Kentucky, in June 1973. This company folded after 14 months of operation, having disappointed its customers by curtailing its product assortment to about 4,000 items (at the time, supermarkets usually carried about 9,000 items).

Why were these attempts to automate the nonstore purchasing of groceries so short-lived, especially given favorable demographic and lifestyle trends? There are four possible explanations:

(1) *Lack of managerial skills*. Each attempt was plagued by a major operational problem. One company could not handle warehousing and logistical problems; another, the computer system; the third, the dynamics of merchandising. The common denominator here is managerial incompetence. These companies simply did not have the managerial skills necessary to run a complex service operation.

(2) *Underfinancing*. Each of the companies was seriously underfinanced. Telemart started from an initial investment base of roughly $2 million; the others, less than $1 million. To imagine that they could develop for only $1 million or $2 million a centralized, mechanized, and computerized distribution system with enough left over for inventory and promotion was, at best, wishful thinking.

(3) *Failure to satisfy consumer needs*. The service was supposed to free shoppers from time-consuming trips to the store. But they had to spend 10 to 30 minutes, depending on the size of their order, compiling a properly coded grocery list from a catalog (and pulling out old invoices if they wanted to compare prices). They had to spend another 10 to 30 minutes giving their orders to the telephone operators or the "talking computer" and then stay home waiting for the groceries to be delivered. Next, they had to examine the quality of the goods and, if necessary, send some of them back for redelivery.

(4) *Inability to offer low prices*. The companies had intended to pass along to consumers the savings resulting from operating economies (e.g., lower rent, lower utility charges, a more efficient warehouse, lower payroll expenses, lower incidence of checkout errors and shoplifting). In reality, consumers paid competitive prices for the items that they ordered as well as a few extra dollars for membership and delivery. In some cases, the membership fee was as much as $10 and the delivery fee $4 per trip.

Mail-order Catalogs

In contrast to the abortive attempts at nonstore grocery shopping, selling through mail-order catalogs positively thrived in the 1970s. Americans spent an estimated $26.2 billion on mail-order items in 1978,[5] up from $12 billion in 1975;[6] over the same period, mail-order houses tallied an average after-tax profit of 7%.[7] These figures compare quite favorably with those of the retailing industry as a whole, whose sales grew at less than half the rate and showed less than half the profit margin of mail-order sales.

In recent years, the fastest growing and most profitable part of the whole mail-order business has been the specialty houses like L.L. Bean, which now account for nearly 75% of total mail-order sales.[8] Their success derives in part from the various factors listed in Table 7.2 and, in part from:

- *Efficient operation*. To support the 26 million catalogs it mails each year, L.L. Bean, for example, is organized so that customers can telephone orders 24 hours a day, 365 days a year, and can return all merchandise without questions asked. The distribution center processes virtually all mail orders within 72 hours, and the computer maintains a sales record on a customer-by-customer basis.

- *Strong financial backing*. Although L.L. Bean is still owned by the Bean family, in recent years an increasing number of corporations with substantial financial resources—corporations such as ITT, Beatrice Foods, W.R. Grace, General Mills, Quaker Oats, and Tenneco—have acquired mail-order businesses. In the future, each of these companies may own several mail-order businesses. General Mills, for example, owns Talbots (women's sportswear), Eddie Bauer (outdoor clothing), Bowers and Ruddy Galleries (rare coins), H.E. Harris (stamps), and Lee Wards (knitting goods).

- *Carefully selected merchandise*. Because a specialty mail-order house knows in detail who its customers are and what they are looking for, it has to carry only a limited assortment of products. The mail-order catalog, in a sense, shops the market for its customers and edits the offering. Selected merchandise simplifies

Table 7.2. **FACTORS CONTRIBUTING TO THE SUCCESS OF MAIL-ORDER CATALOGS**

SOCIOECONOMIC FACTORS	*EXTERNAL FACTORS*	*COMPETITIVE FACTORS*
More women joining the work force	Rising cost of gasoline	Inconvenient store hours
Population growing older	Availability of WATS 800 lines	Unsatisfactory service in stores
Rising discretionary income	Expanded use of credit cards	Difficulty of parking, especially near downtown stores
More single households	Low-cost data processing	"If you can't beat 'em, join 'em" approach of traditional retailers
Growth of the "me" generation	Availability of mailing lists	

things for the customer by eliminating the need to sort through an array of products and by reducing the need for assurance of product quality.

BOUNDED, NOT UNBOUNDED, POTENTIAL

But will this boom in nonstore marketing last? The loss of consumer's discretionary income and a marked decline in their response rates to direct marketing suggest that the 1980s will not be as fertile a decade for continued growth as some observers believe. In our opinion, four primary factors will restrain the growth rate of established methods of nonstore marketing: reluctant consumers, inappropriate products, cautious manufacturers, and threatened retailers.

Reluctant Consumers

For a family living on Manhattan's East Side—especially a family in which both adults work—shopping may be sufficiently tedious to make direct marketing a great convenience. For the many Americans with increasing leisure time, however, shopping is an important form of entertainment. Browsing through a mail-order catalog is simply not as satisfying as being able to touch, feel, and smell the merchandise.

Many consumers see other values in store shopping too. It exposes them to an assortment of product alternatives; it facilitates price comparisons and avoids delivery charges; and it permits consumers to deal personally with salespeople. Although the decline in the quality of in-store service is often cited as one reason for the growth of direct marketing, shoppers still appreciate discussions with store personnel as a source of product information as well as for their social value.

Marketers can, of course, segment consumers according to their preferred shopping styles. Some value convenience more than price and thus respond frequently and enthusiastically to direct marketing offers; some are curious enough about certain kinds of merchandise to pay for information in catalog form. According to an Ogilvy & Mather survey in

1978, the 23% of consumers who spent more than $100 apiece in direct marketing purchases during the previous year accounted for a full 83% of total nonstore dollar volume.[9]

The majority of consumers, however, still view mail and telephone ordering as risky. These people, perhaps remembering the unscrupulous practices of an earlier generation of direct marketers, are less interested in convenience than in product quality, reliable delivery, and the ease with which unsatisfactory products can be returned for refund or replacement. In addition, many view the techniques of direct marketing—the unsolicited telephone calls, the "junk" mail, and the trading and renting of mailing lists—as an invasion of privacy.

Inappropriate Products

Not all products lend themselves equally well to direct marketing. Stereo equipment, for example, is an expensive, heavy, bulky item subject to transit damage and high delivery costs. It requires extensive comparison shopping and in-store demonstration. Even someone who has a specific brand of equipment in mind prefers to purchase it in a store because the retail price of stereo equipment is customarily negotiated at the point-of-sale. And if the equipment must later be returned for exchange or servicing, the typical consumer will perceive a local store as both more convenient and more likely to be responsive than an out-of-state direct marketer.

Nonstore marketers have indeed offered big-ticket luxury items through mail-order catalogs—if only to legitimize in the consumer's mind the idea of purchasing them without visiting a store. A major credit card company, for example, recently offered its cardholders a complete stereo system. Although the system is a well-known brand, recipients of the offer may well have felt that the advertised equipment was shortly to be discontinued or that the credit card company was, at best, a questionable distributor of such equipment. By contrast, when Gulf Oil offers its cardholders a tire inflator, no such doubts or uncertainties exist.

The direct marketing of "collectibles" has enjoyed quite a different consumer response. Collectibles like coins or plates are not especially heavy or bulky, yield high profits relative to transaction and delivery costs, and do not require instructions for use. They are specialty items, often with broad product lines, that by definition are not in wide distribution and sometimes not available at all in stores.

Potential purchasers are price insensitive and lack the strong brand preferences that might prompt extensive comparison shopping. Those direct marketers of collectibles like the Franklin Mint that are able to establish lasting credibility for their company name can significantly reduce a consumer's sense of risk in buying by mail and can therefore amortize the marketing costs of an initial purchase over a sequence of follow-on purchases.

Still other factors can influence the suitability of a product for direct marketing. Health remedies urgently needed by consumers must be distributed through convenience stores; consumers cannot wait for a mail delivery.

Similarly, products that have to be customized do not lend themselves to direct marketing. Neither, of course, do perishable food items. However, these rules do not always hold. Many mail-order companies in Wisconsin market cheeses and cured meats through catalogs because their customers associate the highest quality in cheese with a particular state and are consequently willing to make mail-order purchases to obtain what they obviously view as a specialty item.

From these examples, it should be clear that to date the ideal product for direct marketing has been a small, lightweight yet durable, high-margin specialty item available to consumers only through selective distribution. Direct marketers have with mixed success been attempting to broaden the range of products that consumers are willing to purchase from them by offering free trials, moneyback guarantees, and 800-number toll-free complaint "hotlines." They have also been trying to reduce the consumer's perception of risk by associating an image of quality with their company names.

Cautious Manufacturers

Two principal considerations have kept most manufacturers from engaging in direct marketing themselves, even though it might bring them closer to the consumer and give them more control of distribution channels.

(1) *Opposition from traditional distributors.* With the exception of stores with their own direct marketing operations, retail outlets might view a manufacturer's direct marketing efforts as likely to cut into their own sales. As a result, they might threaten retaliatory action by delisting products or reducing promotional support.

(2) *Limited product lines.* Few manufacturers have sufficiently broad product lines to develop mail-order catalogs of their own. Those manufacturers interested in generating sales through direct marketing, therefore, have to work with a third party. Their products might, say, appear along with those of other manufacturers in a catalog developed by a mail-order house such as Horchow.

If so, however, the manufacturer must be willing both to accept reduced brand-name recognition and to forgo the use of packaging and point-of-sale material to stimulate brand awareness. The manufacturer must also be alert to the threat to its traditional channels of distribution should the direct marketer set a lower price than its retail outlets do.

As a rule, the stronger the manufacturer's relationship with traditional distribution channels and the larger its market share, the less interest the manufacturer will have in nonstore marketing.

Threatened Retailers

As noted previously, direct marketing threatens the sales of traditional retail outlets—especially those that carry high-margin specialty items. Specialty and department stores are not, however, without defense.

Such prestigious department stores as Neiman-Marcus can hedge their bets by becoming direct marketers themselves and thus expand the geographical base of their sales without investing in new stores. They can control the rate at which their nonstore business expands and prevent any reduction in the ROI of their traditional stores.

Chain stores can minimize sales losses by emphasizing personalized in-store service, by extending store hours, by offering in-store boutiques, by developing a specific image for each local outlet, and by competing with the catalogs of direct marketers through newspaper supplement advertising and direct mailings of their own.

Specialty store chains can also compete against direct marketers on the basis of in-store service, convenience, and breadth of assortment. A specialty shoe retailer such as Edison Bros. can offer customers a wide choice of merchandise at different price and quality levels by locating several outlets with different names in a large mall designed for one-stop shopping and by developing more powerful store images through store design and focused product selection.

Because direct marketers require more lead time for product planning than do retailers and because the product mix listed in a catalog cannot be quickly changed, specialty stores that sell fashion-sensitive merchandise are especially well-equipped to compete with direct marketers by emphasizing the up-to-date nature of their product lines.

NEW MARKETING TECHNOLOGIES

For the various reasons mentioned in the preceding sections, we do not foresee as rapid a growth rate during the 1980s for the established techniques of nonstore marketing as some others do. But what will be the impact of the new technologies? Will they really enhance the growth of nonstore marketing by broadening the means by which direct marketers deliver their messages to and accept orders from consumers? In this section, we examine the possibilities opened by three of these new technologies.

Interactive Cable Television

Direct marketers have shown great interest in interactive cable television by purchasing advertising spots and developing new forms of catalog programming. Its appeal to consumers is that it allows them simply to press a keypad to purchase an item that they see advertised on a commercial spot or catalog program rather than having to telephone an 800 number.

A typical catalog program on a cable channel might consist of a 30-minute "fashion show" of a direct marketer's merchandise. Such programs could be shown to all subscribers as a part of regularly scheduled programming or to individual subscribers on request and at their convenience. In fact, Times-Mirror Cable and Comp-U-Card have recently launched in six metropolitan markets "The Shopping Channel," which is exclusively devoted to catalog programming of this nature.

Recent tests of both direct response advertising and catalog programming or interactive cable systems have not, however, been auspicious. Video Communications, Inc. of Tulsa found viewer reaction during a two-hour movie aired on a national cable network to direct response ads for books and furniture to be "practically zero,"[10] and an American Express Co. executive reported that the results of tests of his company's Christmas catalog on the QUBE system "were not overwhelming."[11] Catalog programming on interactive cable television is unlikely either to supplant the printed catalogs used by direct marketers or to emerge in the near future as a significant source of sales revenue for them. There are several reasons for this.

Consumer Barriers

Will people watch catalog programs? Given the range of viewing options, will the drawing power of a catalog program be sufficient to justify both the investment of direct marketers in its production and the investment of cable operators in its transmission? Will consumers be willing to pay more than the regular monthly cable charge for an opportunity to view such programming?

And for those people who do watch a catalog program, what advantages, if any, will it offer them over a printed catalog? Its entertainment value may be high, but will this translate into incremental purchases? Its information value is likely to be higher only when the actual demonstration of a product can add to understanding of its utility.

The printed catalog has several advantages. Readers can put the catalog down or pick it up at any time and can examine some items in detail while skipping others. A consumer often wants to mull over a possible purchase, refer to the catalog entry, and perhaps even discuss it with friends before making a decision.

Such flexibility is less available with catalog programs. If they are a part of regularly scheduled programming, the user must watch them at designated times and make immediate decisions whether to purchase. Not surprisingly, the president of Cable Ad Associates, which recently initiated the development of a national cable catalog, found that "people who didn't have the [printed] catalog wouldn't order. . . . The only way (catalog) marketing on TV will work is through strong print support."[12]

A further deterrent to the purchase of cable-advertised products is the impersonal nature of the transaction. The success of many direct response marketers stems in part from courteous and knowledgeable telephone operators who can respond to questions about the merchandise and in some cases make incremental sales. And though it may eventually be possible for consumers to place an order with a person who will appear on their home TV screen and with whom they can interact directly, such a development is a long way off.

At present, however, even if a shopper is inclined to purchase a cable-advertised item, two other barriers may prevent the transaction from taking place:

First, as with TV advertising, a consumer may be uncertain whether the price of an item is higher than in a store. Some people will be willing to pay more for the convenience of "instant" shopping; others will not. To overcome this price perception problem, many direct marketers indicate in their television advertisements that the products offered are not available in any store.

Second, a consumer may be unwilling to use the electronic funds transfer system (EFTS) that purchasers of catalog program merchandise will use to make payments. With an EFTS, the buyer will not immediately receive a written record of the transaction, will have less opportunity to cancel the transaction than is now possible with payment by check, and will probably lose the advantage of the float. And many people remain concerned about the confidentiality of EFTS transactions and purchases.

Cable Operator Barriers

Like consumers, cable operators may not be very enthusiastic about catalog programming. There are two principal reasons for their lukewarm enthusiasm.

First, cable operators have traditionally focused on obtaining revenues from subscribers, rather than from advertisers, and have been quite sensitive to potential subscriber resentment about inclusion of advertising—even in the form of catalog programming. The idea is likely to become more acceptable as rising costs require cable operators to choose between raising subscription fees and raising advertising revenues.

The introduction of national cable networks such as CNN and ESPN, which are funded by advertising; the establishment of the Cable Advertising Bureau; the development of audience research for cable stations; the growing interest of advertising representatives in handling cable station clients; and the investment in test campaigns by large national advertisers—all these developments suggest that advertising on both one-way and two-way cable television is likely to increase. But if it does, interest in the untried hybrid form, catalog programming, is likely to decrease among both advertisers and station operators.

Second, the public policymakers usually responsible for awarding cable franchises do not always view catalog programming as a positive addition to a prospective franchisee's programming proposals. Indeed, some policymakers may view catalog programming as socially undesirable because disadvantaged consumers may be drawn into making impulse purchases of goods they cannot afford.

Of the roughly 4,500 cable stations in operation in the United States, very few are interactive systems. Of those not interactive in mode, half cannot be converted; and few of the remainder will be converted because cable station franchisees usually enjoy local monopolies. Therefore, no direct marketer can reach all cable television households with a catalog program and an interactive system.

Cost Barriers

The direct marketers whose products are shown on cable programs will have to bear the costs of producing the catalog programs. Some experimentation will be necessary to establish the optimal program format. Unlike a television advertisement, whose costs can be amortized over many showings, a catalog program must absorb the full costs immediately, for it cannot be shown more than a few times in a single market and still be effective.

Usually, local cable station operators pay cable networks, such as Ted Turner's Cable News Network, for the programming that the networks make available. Payments are made on a per subscriber basis, and the station operators cover these payments through their installation and monthly rental charges.

It seems likely, however, that station operators will view catalog programming as a form of advertising and that, far from agreeing to pay for airing it, they will expect compensation themselves. This compensation could take one of two forms: (1) the direct marketer could buy air time for the catalog program in the same way that sponsors now buy spots on television; or (2) the station operator could receive a percentage of the sales revenue generated by orders transmitted through the interactive system.

Even allowing for gradual consumer acceptance of catalog programming, the costs of generating incremental sales dollars are likely to be greater than with direct mail. The relative profitability of catalog programming becomes more questionable still when we consider its possible effect on direct-mail sales. And no direct marketer simultaneously employing both approaches could get away with charging higher prices on the catalog program than in the printed catalog in order to cover the additional costs of catalog programming.

On balance, then, catalog programming on interactive cable television is not ready for widespread adoption as a new direct marketing technique.

Interactive Information Retrieval

Through either the telephone or a two-way interactive cable system, consumers can call up information from computer data banks. The information requested will appear on their television screens. This new technology enables the consumer to control the timing, sequencing, and content of information retrieval and to make purchases of products and services through the use of a keypad, with expenses automatically charged to bank or credit card accounts. Here too, though, several barriers impede the rapid development of a novel approach to direct marketing.

Technological barriers

At present, alphanumerics and graphics, but not still or moving pictures, can be retrieved from a data bank and displayed on a TV screen. Because the system can transmit only verbal, not visual, information on product attributes, it has a built-in constraint: the range of products that a person is likely to buy solely on the basis of information obtained from the system is rather narrow. Other technical problems remain, including the development of an indexing system so that a shopper can identify quickly and easily the best way to call up desired information.

Consumer Barriers

A mass market of shoppers who are at ease with computers will develop only gradually, as children familiar with home video games and classroom computers enter adulthood. To hasten things along, the French government has initiated a 10-year program to eliminate telephone directories. Users must become familiar with computerized data bases and with calling up desired directory information on a video screen attached to every telephone set. Even with greater familiarity, information retrieval systems will require much planning by individual users because they force consumers to seek out product information before deciding whether to make a purchase.

Cost Barriers

Connecting a household to an information retrieval system is expensive; it requires a decoder, a keypad, and/or a specially modified TV set. Since either the consumer or the system operator must shoulder the expense, this investment may be a barrier to acceptance. In addition, each time someone uses the data bank, he or she will incur operating costs. So long as these combined costs hinder mass adoption of the system, its user base will probably remain too small to persuade manufacturers and retailers to supply the necessary data or to absorb some of the cost of including their data in the system.

Other constraints abound. Because of the expense to individual households, European marketers, at least, will initially tailor their information retrieval systems for the business community, supplying it with news, stock market reports, and flight schedules—that is, with time-sensitive and continually changing information. Business executives may use the system, for example, to make hotel reservations or to check on availability of crude oil supplies. And since the business market will lead the consumer market in adopting information retrieval systems, product-related data bases supplied by manufacturers and retailers are unlikely to be an early inclusion. This will certainly be the case in those European countries where government agencies have designed and developed the retrieval systems.

Even if limited product information were included in the data base, would a consumer who uses the system be any more likely to make a purchase than one who receives a mailed catalog? If not, manufacturers and retailers have little incentive to take on the costs of supplying information to the data base.

Nor would a consumer, who can use the system to retrieve information on a range of alternatives in a particular product category, be more likely to make an immediate purchase than, information in hand, to shop one or more stores for a preferred brand. Here too, if the purchase is not made via the system, manufacturers have little incentive to supply information.

But what if a shopper could not only request product information but also ascertain which stores in his area carry a particular product or brand and at what price? Price sensitivity in the marketplace would increase, and the price flexibility of both retailers and manufacturers would decline. Yet for durable goods such as cars and appliances, where prepurchase information might be helpful, price has traditionally been a matter of negotiation between buyer and seller. Thus, it is unlikely to be included in a seller-financed data base. Only those manufacturers and retailers with standardized prices would be prepared to bear the costs of supplying information. Would consumers be willing to pick up the slack?

Videocassettes and Videodiscs

Catalog houses can produce cassettes, or more probably the lower-priced discs, for free distribution or at a nominal charge to households with videocassette recorders or videodisc players. One department store chain has experimented with this approach but has found that it cannot offset the $12 production and delivery costs of a cassette, versus the $2 cost of a printed, mailed catalog, by generating incremental sales.

Because the markets for videocassette recorders and videodisc players now feature several incompatible systems, distribution of a cassette or disc compatible with each consumer's equipment would be a rather complicated process. In addition, high equipment costs, although projected to decline, will delay widespread adoption of this direct marketing system. Standard cassettes and discs might, of course, carry paid commercials as a way of reducing unit costs, but people will probably not enjoy interruptions in their video material and might simply skip the advertisements.

A WORD OF ADVICE

We do not think that these new technologies—cable television, interactive information retrieval, and videocassettes and videodiscs—will accelerate the growth of nonstore marketing. There is little reason to suspect that consumers will soon take to them in large numbers, and they offer direct marketers few, if any, usable techniques for making their selling tasks easier. Nor do we believe that nonstore marketing will soon bring about the predicted revolution in retailing. We do, however, think that the following *evolution* of direct marketing will take place during the next decade:

- The distinction between in-store and nonstore marketing will become even fuzzier than it is now. We expect nonstore marketers to continue expanding their store networks (Avon, for example, recently acquired Tiffany) and retailers to continue expanding their catalog programs (Bloomingdale's recently began to mail its catalogs on an almost monthly basis).

- The established methods of nonstore marketing will continue to dominate the sale of products and services to the consumer, but we expect the rapid growth rate enjoyed by these methods in the 1970s to slow down.

- The actual impact of new technologies on nonstore marketing will be minimal. They will have no major effect on in-home shopping before the year 1990.

As a result, companies already in the direct marketing business, as well as those contemplating entry, should plan to:

- Keep a long time horizon in mind. Successful direct marketers need time to build and refine their businesses and to earn a decent return. A simulation model developed by an industry source concludes that it would take 10 years for an operator of an automated food-shopping system to reach the break-even point.[13]

- Consider the "worst case" scenario in planning by analyzing various "what if" questions and creating contingency plans accordingly. Here are some examples of appropriate questions:

    What if postal rates double?

    What if privacy laws prevent direct marketers from selling or buying mailing lists?

    What if a freeze is placed on credit card usage?

    What if a reputable competitor files for bankruptcy?

    What if consumers mount a revolt against "catalog clutter"?

- Concentrate on establishing efficient and effective operations. As more and more direct marketers compete for the customer's purse, competitive survival will depend on ease of product ordering, high speed and low expense of delivery, intelligent planning of product assortments, inventory levels, catalog mailings, and the quality of customer interaction with the direct marketer.

- Beware of overkill. Consumers who think of catalog browsing as a fascinating pastime may become bored if faced with a blizzard of catalogs.

Nonstore marketers would like to believe that a revolution is under way, but it will come, if at all, more slowly than they expect. It will come only if it can truly satisfy the needs and wants of consumers. Revolutions of this sort are made by consumers, not marketers.

Eight

—————

Point-of-Sale Marketing

———————————————————————————————

The retail point-of-purchase represents the time and place at which all the elements of the sale—the consumer, the money, and the product—come together. By using various communications vehicles, including displays, packaging, sales promotions, in-store advertising, and salespeople, at the point-of-purchase (POP), the marketer hopes to influence the consumer's buying decision.

Partly because of the diversity of communications vehicles available and partly because effective POP programs can aid in competing for retailers' support, marketers need to manage their POP programs carefully so as to ensure that both retailers and consumers will see consistency and coordination in the programs rather than confusion and contradiction. Recent examples of innovative, well-managed POP programs include:

- Atari's Electronic Retail Information Center (ERIC), a computerized display installed in more than 500 stores that is designed to help sell computers. An Atari 800 home computer linked to a videodisc player asks a series of questions to help the retailer determine a customer's level of computer ability and product needs. ERIC then switches on a videodisc that plays the most appropriate of 13 messages based on the customer's inputs.[1]

- Kodak's Disc Camera, launched in May 1982. A rotating display unit presented the disc story to the consumer without the need for salesperson assistance. In addition to the display unit, the POP program included merchandising aids, sales training and meetings for retail store personnel, film display and dispenser units, giant film cartoons, window streamers, lapel buttons, and cash register display cards.[2]

- Ford Motor Company's showroom wine-and-cheese parties, started in Dallas and San Diego in 1982 to provide a "more comfortable [car] buying process for women" and to respond to the fact that 40% of new car purchases (valued at $35 billion) are now made by women. The auto showroom has traditionally been an uncomfortable environment for women, whom salesmen have often patronized or overpowered with technical details. The showroom events represent an effort to manage the point-of-purchase to attract an increasingly important customer segment.[3]

Innovative management of the point-of-purchase has been applied to a broad range of consumer product categories, including:

- Candy, gum, and magazines, which depend on impulse purchases for a large percentage of their sales.

- Personal computers and other new technical products that require in-store demonstration.

- Pantyhose and vitamins, which because they include multiple items in each brand line must be presented especially clearly to the consumer and efficiently stocked.

- Lawn and garden appliances, which are sold through several types of retailers, each of whom requires a different POP program.

- Liquor and tobacco, which are prohibited from advertising in some media.

- Automobiles and other mature, large-ticket items usually associated with intensive personal selling.

We believe that the expenditures of consumer goods manufacturers on POP communications will increase and that marketers who can manage events at the point-of-purchase well can gain competitive advantage. In this chapter we consider why managing the point-of-purchase is becoming more important, the roles of each element of the POP communications mix, and how consumer goods marketers can improve their management of the point-of-purchase.

POP'S NEW IMPORTANCE

POP expenditures are of increasing significance to marketers for three reasons. First, they often prove more productive than advertising and promotion expenditures. Second, the decline in sales support at the store level is stimulating interest among retailers in manufacturers' POP programs. Third, changes in consumers' shopping patterns and expectations, along with an upsurge in impulse buying, mean that the point-of-purchase is playing a more important role in consumers' decision making than ever before.

For the same reasons, retailers are becoming increasingly receptive to manufacturers' offers of POP merchandising programs. Even K Mart stores, long off limits to manufacturers' sales representatives, now allow them to set up displays and offer planograms. The delicate power balance between the manufacturer and the trade is such, however, that retailers will not give up control of the POP readily, particularly at a time when its importance is growing. Moreover, the pressure on retailers to carve out distinctive positionings to survive heightens their determination to control store layouts, space allocations, and POP merchandising.

Hence, at the same time that their interest in manufacturers' POP programs is rising, retailers are becoming more selective than they once were and beginning to impose constraints, such as restricting the height of displays to preserve the vistas in each department and on each floor. To maintain consistency in store formats and to take advantage of volume discounts, Sears, Roebuck and Company recently centralized all fixture ordering at headquarters.

Improving Communications Productivity

Marketers are carefully examining alternatives and supplements to media advertising, which has roughly tripled in cost since 1968. POP programs cannot substitute for media advertising, nor are they as easily controlled in the store since they are implemented on someone else's turf. They can, however, reinforce and remind consumers about the advertising messages they have seen before entering the store. POP programs help improve productivity in the following ways:

- *Low cost.* While reaching 1,000 adults through a 30-second network television commercial costs $4.05 to $7.75, the cost per thousand for a store merchandiser or a sign with a one-year life is only 3 cents to 37 cents.[4] These figures reflect the low production and installation costs of POP materials and the fact that the same POP materials are seen repeatedly by consumers and salespeople.

- *Consumer focus.* POP programs focus on the consumer but also provide a service to the trade. Because they help move products off the shelves into consumers' hands, POP expenditures are often more productive than off-invoice price reductions to the trade, which risk being pocketed and therefore withheld from the consumer.

- *Precise target marketing.* POP programs can be easily tailored to the needs of local markets or classes of trade in response to marketers' increasing emphasis on region-by-region marketing programs and on account management of key retail customers. In addition, particular consumer segments can be precisely targeted. Revlon's Polished Ambers Dermanesse Skin programmer, a non-electronic teaching aid used at the point-of-purchase to suggest appropriate cosmetic combinations to black women, exemplifies a targeted approach that could not be undertaken efficiently via media advertising alone.

- *Easy evaluation*. Alternative POP programs can be inexpensively presented in split samples of stores. Stores equipped with checkout scanner systems can quickly provide the sales data needed to evaluate the impact of POP programs for the benefit of both manufacturer and retailer.

Declining Retail Sales Push

Manufacturers are increasingly questioning whether they can rely on retail sales clerks to push their products at the point-of-purchase. The quality of retail salespeople appears to have declined as their status has diminished. Their high turnover rate (often more than 100% per year) reflects their relatively low educational level and remuneration.

Sales positions are increasingly being viewed as dead-end jobs since more retailers now prefer to hire university-trained managers.

To reduce labor costs and remain price competitive, retailers such as Sears have cut the number of clerks covering the floor in favor of centralized checkouts. Consumers have developed the impression that salespeople are less attentive and knowledgeable when, in fact, they have to cover more shoppers and product lines than before.

To cut costs while extending opening hours, retailers have also shifted to inexperienced and uncommitted part-time salespersons, who often know little about a product's features and cannot demonstrate its use.

Thus, retail salespeople increasingly lack both ability and credibility. Effective POP programs can compensate for such sales weaknesses by enabling the manufacturer to maintain control of the message delivered to the consumer at the place and time of the final purchase decision. Marketers who provide the most attractive, educational, entertaining, and easy-to-use POP programs are likely to win the favor of store management. Their products are also likely to receive more push from overextended retail salespeople because an effective POP program can increase their credibility and facilitate the selling task.

Changing Consumer Expectations

These days consumers are inclined to seek special deals and wait for sales before they buy large ticket items or stock up on small items. As a result, consumer demand for such products as cosmetics and home furnishings fluctuates more widely than ever before. Retailers are interested in POP merchandising techniques and displays that can productively occupy consumers while they are waiting for sales help. For this reason and because of union restrictions on part-time personnel, Bell Phone Centers, for example, offer consumers many POP aids, including demonstration units.

The increasing use of automatic teller machines and vending machines, the expanded use of self-service store formats, and the advent of computerized shopping mall guides all indicate that consumers who value speed and convenience are becoming amenable to helping themselves at the point-of-purchase. This trend is evident, for example, in hardware stores, where manufacturers such as McCulloch and retail chains such as ServiStar are providing more and more display centers to present their product lines.

Many consumers wish to do their shopping quickly and efficiently; yet, at the same time, the longer they are in a retail store, the more likely they are to buy. Purchases planned least often were, according to one survey, auto supplies (94%), magazines and newspapers (91%), and candy and gum (85%).[5] Drugstore purchases, too, were largely unplanned—60% of them, including 78% of snack food and 69% of cosmetics purchases.[6] An average of 39% of department store purchases were unplanned, ranging from 27% of women's lingerie purchases to 62% of costume jewelry purchases.[7] Effective POP programs not only present useful information efficiently; they can also make shopping entertaining and remove some of its frustration.

THE POINT-OF-PURCHASE COMMUNICATIONS MIX

How can consumer goods marketers address the different—and sometimes conflicting—interests of the manufacturer, the retailer, and the consumer at the point-of-purchase?

Using Displays Effectively

For one thing, they can use well-designed displays. They attract consumer attention, facilitate product inspection and selection, allow the access of several shoppers at once, inform and entertain, and stimulate unplanned expenditures. Because additional display space can expand sales without any change in retail price, consumer goods marketers increased their spending on POP displays 12% annually between 1980 and 1982. Well-designed displays respond to the needs of both the retailer and the consumer.

They reduce store labor costs by facilitating shelf stocking and inventory control, minimizing out-of-stock items, and lowering the required level of back-room inventory. For example, automatic feed displays such as 7-Up's single-can dispensers eliminate the need for store clerks to realign shelf stock.

Good displays are designed for a particular type of store and often for a specific store department. For example, the Entenmann Division of General Foods realized that its display designs in the bakery sections of supermarkets were not transferable to the cash register areas, where the company wished to sell its new line of snacks, so it developed an additional range of displays.

Good displays reflect the likely level of trade support. There is no point in designing a large display that will not generate the retailer's required level of inventory turnover. Likewise, there is no point in offering the trade a permanent display for a seasonal product. Richardson-Vicks, for example, redesigns its display each year rather than provide a permanent fixture because retailers give floor space to Vicks Cold Centers during the winter months only.

Well-designed displays are versatile and can accommodate new products. Max Factor, for example, provides retailers with a floor-stand display consisting of a series of interchangeable trays and cartridges. New product lines, packed in similar trays, can be easily inserted, while the cartridges can, when removed from the floor stand, double as counter display units.

Manufacturers must, of course, also keep their own interests in mind when they are designing displays. For example, Johnson & Johnson's First Aid Center provides supermarkets and drugstores with a permanent display for more than 30 of its first aid items.[8] By creating a strong visual impact at the point-of-purchase, the display presents Johnson & Johnson as a large, well-established company that offers consumers the convenience of easy product selection and "one-shelf shopping" for all their first aid needs. It also discourages retailers from stocking only the fastest-moving items. In addition, the display carries the company name and thus prevents the retailers from using the display to stock other products. At the same time, it helps Johnson & Johnson preempt competition in slow-moving product categories in which the retailer can justify stocking only one brand.

While displays such as these are becoming prevalent in self-service environments, other innovative displays are being developed to supplement the efforts of salespeople. For example, Mannington Mills' Compu-Flor, a small computerized display placed in floor covering retail outlets, is programmed to use a potential consumer's answers to eight questions about room decor. The terminal then displays three to ten appropriate Mannington styles for the customer to choose from. When idle, the machine beeps periodically to attract consumers. Mannington had placed the units in 700 stores by the end of 1982 at a cost of $8 million, an amount equal to the company's advertising budget.

Mannington found that Compu-Flor selected styles for customers more efficiently than salespeople (who had trouble remembering all the styles in the product line), encouraged salespeople to push Mannington products rather than those of its two larger competitors (Armstrong and

Congoleum), and boosted the number of sales closed on a customer's first store visit.[9]

Compu-Flor is just one of a number of computerized video displays at the point-of-purchase that provide a standard controllable message from manufacturer to consumer, a way of engaging customers' attention while they are waiting for·sales assistance, and entertainment.

A Package Is More Than a Container

Packaging has many functions beyond acting as a container for a product.

Appropriate packaging, of course, attracts attention at the point-of-purchase. Manufacturers such as Nabisco and Kellogg use the same package design for many items in their product lines to present a highly visible billboard of packages to consumers at the point-of-purchase. In 1979, Nabisco standardized the package design of its chocolate-covered cookies; the market share for this product rose from 24% to 34% by 1981.[10]

Standardized packaging also permits easy identification of brands, types, and sizes. Private-label suppliers have imitated the color codes used to identify various sizes of disposable diapers made by the brand name manufacturers. Similarly, packaging communicates product benefits and identifies target groups. Contrast the packaging of Marlboro cigarettes, aimed at men, Virginia Slims, targeted at women, and Benson & Hedges Deluxe Ultra Lights, with a silver package designed to appeal to elitists among both men and women.

And the right packaging limits the potential for pilferage of small items. The manufacturer of Fevertest, a plastic strip that, when placed on the forehead, indicates the presence of fever, added size and value to the product by enclosing the strip in a wallet, packaging the wallet in a blister pack, and displaying the item on pegboards at supermarket and drugstore checkout counters.

Consumer and trade expectations of product packaging should not discourage marketers from innovation, though frequent changes in package size and design breed trade resistance, especially when existing shelf configurations cannot easily accommodate the new packages. Reflecting the shift to self-service car maintenance, Kendall and Arco recently began to sell oil in plastic containers with built-in pouring spouts.

Making Shopping Fun

Manufacturers are increasingly using consumer promotions to make shopping exciting. These include premiums, coupons, samples, and refund offers in or on product packages to help them stand out and break through the visual clutter at the point-of-purchase. Package-delivered promotions have the further advantage of being inexpensive in comparison with consumer promotions offered in magazine advertisements or direct mail campaigns.

Manufacturers are also becoming aware that retailers favor manufacturers whose promotions bring consumers into the store. For example, some sweepstakes promotions, such as Brown Shoe Company's Footworks contest, encourage the consumer to match symbols in an advertisement with those on a store display or package in order to enter the contest. Retailers also like promotions that tie into store merchandising themes and cross-sell other products (promotions built around recipes or complete home decorating services, for instance) and promotions that avoid the use of special price packs that require retailers to replace existing shelf stock and set up new Universal Product Code entries in store computer systems.

In-store Advertising Media

Manufacturers can extend to retailers a number of innovative approaches for reinforcing brand awareness and delivering advertising messages at the point-of-purchase. These include:

- Commercials broadcast over in-store sound systems.
- Moving message display units with changeable electronic messages.

- Customer-activated videotapes and videodiscs that show merchandise such as furniture that is too bulky to be displayed on the department floor; the videotapes can also be played in window displays to present, for example, designer fashion shows.

- Television sets installed over cash registers to show waiting customers commercials for products that are usually available nearby.

- Advertisements on carts used in supermarkets and other self-service outlets.

- Danglers and mobile displays that use available air space rather than limited floor space.

IMPLEMENTATION STEPS

Recognizing the significance of the point-of-purchase is not enough. Consumer goods marketers must pay more attention to developing effective POP programs and, even more important, to ensuring that they are properly implemented at the store level.

Before developing a POP program, managers must have a clear understanding of their marketing strategy—which products are being delivered to which markets through which channels of distribution. Given the marketing strategy, marketers should go on to answer such questions as:

- What must happen at the point-of-purchase to satisfy consumer needs?

- Which channel members—manufacturers, retailers, consumers— are willing to perform which functions?

- Which members can perform them most cost-effectively?

- How should the functions be allocated?

- How should the pricing structure for the product (and for the POP program) reflect this allocation of functions?

Program Development

Once they answer these questions, marketers can work out the specifics of the POP program—objectives, vehicles, and budgets. Here are five principles that should guide this process:

(1) Integrate all elements of the POP communications mix. The package, for example, cannot be designed independently of the display. All POP vehicles should communicate consistent and mutually reinforcing messages to both the trade and the consumer.

(2) Offer the trade a coordinated POP program for an entire product line rather than a collection of POP materials for particular items. To further impress the trade, make sure that the POP program is easy to understand and financially realistic.

(3) Link POP assistance to trade performance. High-quality displays, for example, should not be given away to the trade unless linked to a quantity purchase or paid for with cooperative advertising dollars earned on previous purchases.

(4) Assume that various POP programs will be necessary for distribution channels. The traditional hardware store and the self-service mass merchandiser, for example, differ both in store environment and in type of customer; the ideal POP program for each will not be the same.

(5) Integrate POP communications with non-POP communications. Television advertising should tell consumers in which stores and departments they can find the advertised product and should include shots of product packages and displays to facilitate consumer recall and brand identification at the point-of-purchase. Sometimes a POP display becomes the basis for a television advertising campaign, as in the case of the Uniroyal POP unit, which invited the consumer to drill a hole in a Royal Seal tire to demonstrate that no air was lost if it was punctured.

Program Execution

Any POP program is only as effective as the quality of its implementation at the store level. Effective implementation requires that managers, first, recognize the execution challenge. Many innovative approaches to managing the point-of-purchase fail because responsibilities for such tasks as stocking and maintaining displays are not clearly allocated or, once allocated, are not properly performed. Under these circumstances, cooperation between manufacturers and retailers can quickly turn into recrimination.

Consumer goods marketers are often too eager to assume POP responsibilities themselves. To increase their control over the execution of their marketing programs, they might enhance effectiveness and reduce expense to make the programs work by appropriately compensating the retailers.

Two recent examples highlight the risks of ineffective execution at the point-of-purchase:

- General Entertainment Corporation failed in its 1982 attempt to market popular music cassette tapes from floor-stand displays in supermarkets partly because its field sales force could not maintain display inventories of 168 stockkeeping units, many of which changed every few months.

- Binney & Smith, manufacturer of Crayola crayons and other arts materials, quickly placed 1,500 special merchandising units called Crayola Fun Centers in a variety of distribution outlets following their introduction in 1980. But efficiently servicing the displays proved difficult, and Binney terminated the contract of the servicing firm handling this task.

In general, the greater the number of stockkeeping units in a display and the greater the diversity of channel environments in which the displays are placed, the more complex and challenging effective execution becomes.

Next, managers must evaluate the execution alternatives. Consumer goods marketers usually have three options for carrying out POP programs—to use their own salespeople, to contract with brokers or service merchandisers, and to rely on the retailer. The evaluation should center on comparative costs, degree of marketers' control over the execution, and the relative importance of effective POP merchandising in leveraging a product's overall marketing program. The more important it is, the more justification the marketer has for using a direct sales force.

One important reason for the success of L'eggs was the company's decision to have its own salespeople deliver the product on consignment to stores and to assume total responsibility for managing the point-of-purchase. Yet the ability of the L'eggs salespeople to stock product displays efficiently had a negative twist; although it enabled L'eggs to introduce numerous line extensions, their addition complicated the product selection process at the point-of-purchase and made it seem inconvenient in the minds of many consumers.

To ensure the freshness and integrity of its snacks, Frito-Lay's 9,000 van salespeople visit 300,000 outlets each week. Beyond taking orders, they are trained to advise retailers about how to allocate shelf space in the snack food section according to a six-point space management program. Yet, despite the clout of its sales force, Frito-Lay could not persuade supermarkets to stock its new line of Grandma's cookies at supermarket checkout counters; they are now being displayed in the cookie sections.

These two examples deliver an important message. Even when a company has the sales force to ensure the execution of a POP program, it must never lose sight of the needs of consumers and the trade.

Many consumer goods marketers cannot afford their own sales forces and must rely on brokers or service merchandisers. Both are often unfairly demeaned. A good broker is sometimes more effective than a direct sales force in managing the point-of-purchase, as many big companies, including H.J. Heinz and Pillsbury, know well. Because they carry a number of noncompeting product lines, brokers enjoy economies of scale that enable them to visit retail stores more often than a manufacturer's sales force to check stocks, reset displays, and offer planograms. Brokers can establish close relationships with retailers in their local areas and organize blockbuster promotional events for their principals. For frozen food manufacturers, brokers are especially important to managing the point-of-purchase. Frequent store visits are essential because freezer space is limited on account of equipment and energy costs, and stores carry little, if any, back-room inventory.

If your company uses brokers or service merchandisers, here are four approaches to ensure that they effectively execute your POP program:

(1) Check the size of the broker's sales force against the company's product line commitments. Is the brokerage firm overextended? How important is your business to the firm?

(2) Develop a POP program that is creative yet easy to implement. As a result, your company may gain more attention from the broker's salespeople (and, therefore, the trade) than the broker's other principals.

(3) Compensate the broker appropriately for the POP tasks you expect him or her to perform. Do you provide bonus incentives to broker salespeople for additional display placements?

(4) Evaluate POP performance. Do you buy display audits to compare your share of display space with your market share? Do you occasionally play the customer, visit stores, check displays, and ask sales clerks for information?

These same principles are relevant whether the retailer, a broker, or a direct sales force is responsible for executing the POP program. The most important point for the consumer goods marketer to recognize is that an effective POP program never runs like clockwork. It needs constant attention and reevaluation.

Many consumer goods marketers are increasing their expenditures on POP programs. In 1982, for example, Elizabeth Arden, Inc. raised its POP budget by 40%.[11] What these marketers recognize is the old adage that the difference between success and failure often depends on the last 5% of effort rather than on the 95% that preceded it. In consumer marketing, that last 5% manifests itself at the point-of-purchase just before consumers choose what to buy.

Nine

_____

Promotion and Advertising

The increasing use of price promotions has aroused strong concern among many marketers. They argue that price promotions reduce the potential of other elements of the marketing mix by bleeding the advertising budget, decreasing brand loyalty, increasing consumer price sensitivity, and contributing to an excessive managerial focus on short-term sales and earnings.

We believe that some of these trends are inherent in today's marketplace, and that interest in price promotions is a *response* to them, not their cause. Price promotions—short-term incentives directed at the trade and/or the end consumers—can offer marketers substantial benefits, some of them not available through other marketing tools. Used effectively, they can enable small companies to challenge large competitors, reduce the risk of first-time purchase for consumers and retailers, and stimulate consumer demand. Perhaps most important, price promotions allow manufacturers to adjust to supply and demand fluctuations by using demand pricing, or charging different market segments different prices for the same product.

Price promotion is being heavily criticized partly because accounting procedures typically exaggerate its costs and undervalue its contribution. This chapter will focus on the general characteristics of price promotions, the specific value of demand pricing, and the proper evaluation of price promotion costs.

THE PROMOTION DEBATE

There is no doubt that the use of price promotions has increased more rapidly than the use of advertising in recent years.[1] Forces causing the growth include the following.

- Slow population growth, combined with excess manufacturing and retail capacity, has intensified competition for market share. Promotions can achieve short-term increases in sales, market share, and capacity utilization.

- Fragmented consumer audiences and media-cost inflation have made advertising harder to manage.

- As product categories mature, opportunities for product differentiation decrease, good advertising copy becomes harder to develop, the quality gap between private labels and national brands narrows, and pressure for price promotions increases.

- Regional trade concentration, computerized sales data collected at the point-of-sale, and the increasing professionalism of retail management are adding to the trade's power and putting pressure on manufacturers for more deals.

- Mergers, acquisitions, and the securities industry have placed more pressure on top management to focus on short-term earnings. Price promotions boost short-term sales more assuredly than advertising does.

The airline industry is a good example of these forces at work. In 1985, 86% of all seats sold by the twelve major U.S. carriers were sold at a discount (average discount of 44%), compared to only 56% in 1980. Excess capacity following deregulation resulted in only 62% of all seats being filled in 1985. Falling fuel prices, high fixed costs, and the inherent inability to inventory excess seats further encourage discounting. Computerized reservation systems can quickly implement fare changes and make it easy for competitors to respond.

The airline example also shows how the growth in promotion expenditures is partly artificial. A large proportion of promotion expenditures in the airline industry represents adjustments to artificially high list prices rather than genuine merchandising efforts.

Yet promotion continues to be seen as a *cause* of problems rather than a *symptom*, particularly by advertising executives who see the growth of promotion as a threat. Very often, promotion is blamed for the following trends.

- *Decreasing brand loyalty.* The inability of manufacturers to develop truly differentiated products and the proliferation of me-too products and line extensions are more basic causes of brand switching than promotion. The auto industry is a good example.

- *Increasing price sensitivity.* Although consumer responsiveness to promotions has been found to correlate with price sensitivity, this is a chicken and egg question.[2] The recessions of the 1970s and the early 1980s were at least as responsible as the proliferation of manufacturers' deals for programming many consumers to buy only on deal.

- *Detracting from a quality image.* So many products are now offered on deal that a product's image is unlikely to be hurt by promotion, particularly if the regular list price is recognized as artificially high; if the promotion is an annual event accepted by consumers, such as a year-end clearance sale; if the other elements of the marketing mix (such as the advertising, packaging, and distribution channels) testify to product quality; and if independent sources such as *Consumer Reports* give the product high marks.

- *Focusing management on the short term.* In fact, a short-term orientation, driven by top management's emphasis on quarterly results, is the *cause* rather than the result of promotions used to boost sales. A recent study indicated that 90% of product managers would rather spend less time on short-term promotion and more time on franchise-building advertising, but the top-rated managers were those who spent more time on promotion, indicating that senior management is rewarding a short-term orientation.[3]

BENEFITS OF PROMOTIONS

Not only are the cause-and-effect relationships between these four trends and price promotions often confused, but there are also many benefits of price promotions for manufacturers, retail trade, and consumers that are often overlooked. These include the following.

- Price promotions enable manufacturers to adjust to variations in supply and demand without changing list prices. Often price promotions can help even out peaks and valleys in consumer demand to lower average operating costs. In addition, list prices are often set high as a defense against price controls, rapid increases in commodity prices, or to test "how high is up" in sustainable price levels.

- Because price promotion costs are variable with volume, they enable small, regional businesses to compete against brands with large advertising budgets. The same "pay as you go" aspect of promotions permits the survival of new products targeted at segments too small to warrant mass media advertising.

- By inducing consumer trial of new products and clearing retail inventories of obsolete products, price promotions reduce the retailer's risk in stocking new brands. This fact allows these brands to get consumer exposure faster than otherwise would be the case (though promotions can also help marketers of existing products defend against new brands by loading inventories).

- Price promotions encourage different retail formats, thereby increasing consumer choice. Because different items are on promotion weekly, consumer choice is enhanced, and shopping for otherwise mundane products becomes more exciting.

- Price promotions may increase consumer demand by encouraging trial in new categories and by improving the attention-getting power of advertising. Many promotions, especially coupons and premiums, convey product benefits as well as price information. Awareness and knowledge of prices may be improved by price promotion activity.

- Buying on deal is a simple rule for time-pressured consumers; many of them derive satisfaction from being smart shoppers, taking advantage of price specials, and redeeming coupons.

PRICE PROMOTION AS DEMAND PRICING

An additional benefit of promotion—one that has received more attention from academics than from managers and is the focus of the remainder of this chapter—is its value in implementing demand pricing.[4] *Demand pricing* means charging different market segments different prices for the same product or service. In this context, segments can mean different groups of purchasers as well as different purchasing situations with respect to time, place, and conditions of sale.

There are three reasons that demand pricing is an increasingly important aspect of price promotion.

- There is increasing *segmentation* in consumer markets. These segments differ in their price and promotion sensitivities. A segment of price-insensitive dual-income households can be contrasted to a segment of price-sensitive and deal-prone consumers in fixed-income households whose purchasing power is not rising nearly so fast.

- This consumer segmentation is reflected in the proliferation of *new retail formats*, ranging from limited-assortment club warehouse stores to gourmet superstores, each with a different price-quality positioning. Demand pricing can be directed at classes of trade and individual trade accounts as well as at consumers.

- The emergence of *specialized media* vehicles such as regional magazines and focused cable TV, as well as direct mail, permits promotions to be targeted at specific segments with less leakage.

The concept of demand pricing applies to both "permanent" pricing structures and "temporary" price promotions. For example, early payment discounts are a permanent feature of pricing policies that offer lower prices to those paying promptly. Quantity discounts are also permanent pricing policies that may offer lower prices to one segment than to another.

Charging different prices to different segments will not be more profitable than charging everyone a single price unless the following conditions apply.

- The segments must be separated, or separable to some degree. For example, charging lower telephone rates on weekends encourages consumers to place more personal calls on weekends and also helps telephone companies to even out demand. However, business and personal callers are not perfectly separated; some consumers continue to place personal calls during peak hours, and others would have called on weekends anyway at the peak rate.

- The segments must have different price elasticities and/or different variable costs (or opportunity costs). Segments will have different optimal prices if either price-quantity relationships are different and the variable costs are the same, or vice versa. (If *both* elasticities and costs are different, the effects could cancel or amplify each other. For example, refrigerators may be worth less to Eskimos, but if it costs more to ship refrigerators a great distance, then you could still be forced to charge Eskimos more than you would mainland customers.)

Under comparable circumstances, demand pricing is more profitable when it is difficult for customers in one segment to buy at the price offered to another segment—in other words, when there is minimal "leakage."[5] Therefore, services that cannot be inventoried and are difficult to transfer, such as hotel rooms, can have widely different prices. On the other hand, most products can be inventoried and resold, so when manufacturers run regional price promotions, it is possible for trade customers to buy more than they need and divert the excess to other markets. Other examples of leakage are mistargeting in direct-mail coupon drops and broker trading in airline coupons that enables business travelers to take advantage of rates intended for vacationers.

A major benefit of price promotions to marketers is the ability to price discriminate (in the economic sense of the word) among segments on a temporary basis. Whether a price promotion can *separate markets* is key to its profitability, however. Natural separation of markets occurs as a result of geographic distance between segments, lack of communication between segments, the passage of time, and in international markets, different taxes and duties. Marketers increase or decrease the separation of markets with slight product modifications, separate sales forces, policies with respect to freight charges, and other pricing decisions.*

Passive vs. Active Price Discrimination

"Passive" price discrimination occurs when a lower price is available to a purchaser, but the purchaser chooses not to expend the effort to take

---

*For example, quoting "delivered" instead of FOB prices can make it harder to compare net prices.

advantage of it. We do not question the right to a slightly better "deal" on a Porsche if someone is willing to travel to Germany, buy the car, and cope with shipping it back to the United States. In the same way, we acknowledge that consumers who go to the trouble of clipping, saving, and redeeming coupons should receive a price break.

"Active" price discrimination occurs when marketers restrict the availability of a special price to a certain occasion or group of consumers. Examples of active price discrimination include senior citizen discounts and regional price promotions.

Two-Step Price Discrimination

In the case of trade discounts that may or may not be passed along to consumers, the distinction between active and passive price discrimination is even more difficult to make. Such discounts, although offered to the trade, not the consumer, can result in more price-sensitive consumers being offered lower retail prices through a two-step process.

Certain trade accounts buy more than their normal inventory to take advantage of manufacturer deals (forward buy) and thereby achieve lower average prices than accounts that do not. Some trade accounts—notably warehouse stores and club stores—forgo continuity of assortment in favor of buying *only* deal merchandise. The result is that some chains buy a larger percentage of their total merchandise on deal than do others. Many of these stores appeal to the more price-sensitive consumers in their local trading areas. Thus *temporary* trade discounts can allow stores with the most price-sensitive customers to achieve the lowest average prices over the entire year and permit demand pricing at the consumer level.

Even though equivalent prices may be offered to all trade accounts, passive price discrimination at both the trade and consumer levels occurs because not all retailers choose to take advantage of trade deals and not all consumers choose to shop at the chains that offer the lowest prices.

Profit Gains from Demand Pricing

Demand pricing can increase profits even when only "leaky" forms of market separation are possible. Calculating the profitability of demand pricing is a conceptually simple process that requires specific assumptions about the following:

- The marginal cost (principally variable cost) of supplying each segment;
- The demand function (price versus quantity relationships) of each segment;
- The degree to which leakage occurs; and
- The cost of the separation (such as the costs of printing and distributing coupons and of implementing trade promotions, rebates, and similar programs).

Standard spreadsheet models can be used for the analysis, even with a variety of assumptions about the four factors. In the next example only two segments are considered, but there is no reason either in theory or practice that more could not be analyzed using the same process.

Table 9.1 shows disguised data for a shampoo brand targeted at two distinct consumer segments. The list-price segment—the adult market—is relatively price insensitive and the promotion segment—the teenager market—is price sensitive. The variable cost of supplying each unit is $.80 per unit. The optimal price for the list-price segment, if one could perfectly separate it from the promotion segment, would be $2.00, and the optimal price for the promotion segment would be $1.40. If the segments could not be separated, the optimal single price would be $1.60.

Column 1 assumes a single-price strategy. Column 2 shows the expected contribution for a "perfect" or zero leakage dual-price strategy. Column 3 allows for 20% leakage and calculates volume and contribution for a dual-price strategy. The "units" line reflects the fact that the number of units sold will go up as prices go down.

Table 9.1. CONTRIBUTION FROM PRICE PROMOTION STRATEGY VS. SINGLE-PRICE STRATEGY

	COLUMN 1	COLUMN 2		COLUMN 3	
	SINGLE-PRICE	DUAL-PRICE LEAKAGE = 0		DUAL-PRICE LEAKAGE = 20%	
	List	List	Promotion	List	Promotion
PRICE	$1.60	$2.00	$1.40	$2.00	$1.40
UNITS	140.00	70.00	90.00	56.00	89.00
AVERAGE UNIT PRICE	$1.60	$1.63		$1.61	
UNIT VARIABLE COST	.80	.80		.80	
AVERAGE UNIT MARGIN	.80	.83		.81	
TOTAL NUMBER OF UNITS	140.00	160.00		145.00	
TOTAL CONTRIBUTION	$112.00	$138.00		$120.60	
PROMOTION ADMINISTRATION (2%)	.00	($6.50)		($5.80)	
NET CONTRIBUTION	$112.00	$131.50		$114.80	
GAIN FROM PROMOTION	—	$19.50		$2.80	
ADVERTISING	$20.00	$20.00		$20.00	
PROMOTION/GROSS SALES	0%	21%		19%	
ADVERTISING/GROSS SALES	9%	7%		6%	
ADVERTISING/PROMOTION	100:0	25:75		25:75	

To illustrate "leakage," we have assumed that 20% of the list-price segment would buy 17 units at the promotion price of $1.40 (20% of 85 = 17) and that 80% of the promotion-price segment would buy 72 units (80% of 90 = 72) at the promotion price.* Sales at list price would come only from the list-price segment (80% of 70 = 56) because, at the list price of $2.00, demand in the promotion-price segment would be zero. Total promotion unit sales are 89 (17 + 72) and list-price unit sales are 56 (56 + 0). The unit sales to each segment at a given price are shown in Table 9.2.

Controlling Leakage

Leakage reduces profits when consumers who are not targeted to receive a promotion price manage to take advantage of it, or when those who should have received a promotion price do not. However, as Column 2 in Table 9.1 illustrates, the net effect of price promotions on contribution to profit can still be positive even with substantial leakage. Nevertheless, managers should do the following to reduce leakage.

- Research the price sensitivities and the variable costs of serving various market segments and analyze the differences.

- Take a "rifle shot" approach to targeting announcements of price discounts through media that will selectively reach more price-sensitive consumers or those for whom the variable costs (sometimes opportunity costs) are lowest. Direct mail delivery of consumer promotion offers is especially appropriate.

- Attach restrictions and qualifiers to promotions offering the largest discounts, as the airlines do, so that only the most price-sensitive consumers will expend the effort to obtain them.

- Enforce merchandising performance requirements that assure pass-through of trade allowances to consumers and minimize the leakage that results from forward buying by retailers and from the diversion of goods to other geographic markets or discounters.

*The remaining 20% of the promotion price segment is not aware of the promotion price.

Table 9.2. PRICE, QUANTITY, AND CONTRIBUTION* RELATIONSHIPS FOR LIST-PRICE AND PROMOTION-PRICE SEGMENTS

Price	LIST-PRICE SEGMENT		PROMOTION-PRICE SEGMENT		TOTAL MARKET (LIST + PROMOTION)	
	Units	Contribution†	Units	Contribution	Units	Contribution
$2.00	70.0	$84.00	0	$.00	70.0	$84.00
1.90	72.5	79.75	15.0	16.50	87.5	96.25
1.80	75.0	75.00	30.0	30.00	105.0	105.00
1.70	77.5	69.75	45.0	40.50	122.5	110.25
1.60	80.0	64.00	60.0	48.00	140.0	112.00
1.50	82.5	57.75	75.0	52.50	157.5	110.25
1.40	85.0	51.00	90.0	54.00	175.0	105.00

*Contribution based on variable unit cost of $.80.

†To be read: At a price of $2.00, the list-price segment would buy 70 units, producing a contribution of $84.00 (= 70 units × [2.00 − .80]).

Improving Price Promotion Costing

A few years ago—when price promotion expenditures amounted to only 1% of sales—assessing the profitability of promotions, calculating the level of leakage, and choosing costing procedures for promotions were relatively unimportant. However, now that promotion expenditures are often ten times that amount, managers need to understand the methods used to assess the cost of price promotions. We believe that many companies are using costing methods heavily biased against price promotions in situations where demand pricing effects are substantial. The bias stems from using artificially high list prices for cost calculations.

The current method of calculating the amount spent for price promotions is as follows:

> The discount offered per unit from list price is multiplied by the number of units sold on promotion. To this figure is added the costs of implementing the promotion, such as printing coupons, manufacturing special packages, and, in some cases, advertising the promotion. Summing these costs for each trade and consumer promotion yields the total amount allocated to price promotions.

List price for such calculations is typically the highest price charged. In our example, the costing process would show high costs of price promotions as a percentage of sales, and more than half of all units would be sold on deal. However, the effect of price promotions on profits would be positive, not negative.

Estimating the "cost" of promotions in this way assumes that the *optimal list price would be just as high if promotions were not run*. However, this assumption is not valid when price promotions help separate the market into price-sensitive and less price-sensitive segments. Under these circumstances the optimal list prices when promotions can be offered is higher than the list price under a single-price policy. We believe that, in calculating the cost of promotions, the appropriate list price to use is the price that *would be charged* under a no-promotion policy.

Using the example in Table 9.1, if price discounts were not offered, the optimal price would be $1.60. The cost of price discounts should be calculated against the $1.60 price. The $2.00 price should be charged only if promotions are used. Using the higher list prices makes promotions appear to cost more. Also, the budget should receive "credits" for sales at prices "higher than list" ($2.00 − $1.60 = + $.40 per unit). In some situations, the net effect of running a price promotion could be a credit, not a debit.

In fact, such a situation applies in our example. The actual average price received is higher with price promotions than without. Of course, not all situations yield such a result. Notice that the average price obtained is higher per unit *and* that more units are sold with price promotions than without. How, then, can a cost be associated with the price promotions?

The cost of administering promotions in marketing management and sales force time may be significant. In addition, there are incremental production and logistics costs to consider. Combined, these may amount to as much as 2% of sales. The more complicated the promotion policy, the higher the administration costs. However, the costs of a one-price strategy may be higher in terms of opportunities forgone. Also, well-executed price promotions will have less leakage across segments and, therefore, more profitability.

Managers should avoid using incorrect costing procedures for price promotions because they can have the following undesirable consequences.

- Artificial concern is generated over apparently increasing expenditures for promotion; and by comparison, advertising appears to suffer. In fact, advertising expenditures may not have changed.

- If the budgeting process is to first establish the size of the marketing budget and then allocate shares to advertising and promotion, promotion costs could be overestimated and advertising could be *wrongly* reduced as a result.

- If sales figures are based on list prices, increasing promotion would cause gross sales to increase faster than either unit sales or net sales after promotion discounts. Of course, such increases would be mainly accounting artifacts.

IMPLICATIONS

Price promotions are a symptom, not the cause, of the many phenomena for which they are blamed. We believe that the current emphasis on returning to pull marketing risks overlooking the many benefits of price promotions. One key benefit is promotion's use in implementing demand pricing or price discrimination policies that generate long-term volume and profits. We believe that this benefit is being undervalued by the use of inappropriate costing practices that make promotions appear more expensive than they are, reduce the incentive to use them, and inflate their apparent share of the marketing budget. When variations in marginal costs, administrative costs of promotions, relative price elasticity of the segments, and "leakage" between segments are all considered, the use of price promotions will frequently be more profitable than a single-price policy.

Ten

Marketing Organization

PRESSURE ON THE SYSTEM

Why are product managers under more time pressure? Why is the job more complex than ever before?

- With annual population growth running at only 0.8%, many consumer goods companies are trying to increase sales by capturing market share through new products targeted at narrow market segments rather than at the mass market. Reflecting greater demographic heterogeneity, the consumer marketplace that the product manager has to deal with is becoming more fragmented and complex as a result.

- At the same time, more concentrated and sophisticated channels of distribution are now equipped with product movement information from retail check-out scanners and are in a stronger bargaining position with manufacturers than ever before.[1] To secure shelf space for their new products, today's product managers therefore have to be as adept at push marketing and sales promotion to the trade as they are at developing consumer advertising to pull their products through the channel.[2]

- As maturing markets with slow volume growth prompt manufacturers to explore new distribution channels, product managers now have to develop different marketing programs for different classes of trade from grocery superstores to mass merchandisers.

- Likewise, today's product manager is expected to adapt the national marketing program from one geographic market to another market to reflect regional differences in the product's competitive strength. Campbell Soup and General Foods are just two of many companies emphasizing regional marketing.[3,4]

- As marketing itself becomes more complex, the generalist product manager is in increasing need of help from staff for specialized information. For example, media audience fragmentation and a proliferation of alternative media vehicles are making media budgeting more challenging.[5] Scanner panel data and new research techniques are adding to the market research burden. Impulse purchasing is increasing and adding to the importance of package design and point-of-sale merchandising.[6]

- To boost margins in a slow growth environment, product managers are having to spend more time working closely with manufacturing and product design to reduce unit costs.

- At the same time, product life cycles are shortening and today's product manager is being asked to search harder than ever for new market niches and product opportunities. But there is insufficient time for creative thinking, and both career security and pressure from top management for quick results to improve quarterly earnings dissuade product managers from attacking new product development opportunities other than safe line extensions.*

*Initiatives Group forecast 5,200 new consumer product introductions in 1986 but noted that the vast majority would be line extensions.

At the same time that the demands on the product manager's time are increasing, slower sales growth and the resulting desire of manufacturers to control costs are making top management reluctant to add product management personnel and marketing support staff. Some senior marketers may argue that the best product managers will still be able to figure out what drives their businesses, allocate their time accordingly, and be successful. However, task complexity has increased to the point that such a hands-off approach can now occur only at the price of more frustration, higher turnover, and lower productivity. The information generated by a product management audit can help to prevent these problems.

WHY DO AN AUDIT?

The product management audit we have developed focuses on time allocation. It gathers survey data on how product management personnel allocate their working time among various *job content* and *job process* categories. Job content refers to different functional activities such as advertising and product development. Job process encompasses activities such as writing reports, making presentations, and analyzing data. The major categories of job content and job process are listed in Tables 10.1 and 10.2, which are taken directly from the audit questionnaire.

The principal benefits that companies with product management systems can gain from the audit include the following:

(1) *Managing change.* As was indicated above, the environment in which the product manager is operating is changing dramatically. The audit permits top managers to take a detailed snapshot of the product manager's job, to see how radically it has changed since they were product managers, and to determine how it should be altered to respond both to the changing environment and to their vision of what the job should be. In particular, the audit can help top management to determine whether product management personnel are spending enough time on the tasks that really drive business growth.

Table 10.1. JOB CONTENT CATEGORIES

1. *Advertising*
   a. Media
   b. Copy Development
   c. Copy Production
   d. Management and/or Legal Approval
   e. Other

2. *Trade Promotion*
   a. Design
   b. Copy Development (e.g. POP)
   c. Execution
   d. Evaluation
   e. Other

3. *Consumer Promotion*
   a. Design
   b. Copy Development (e.g. FSIs, Sunday Supplement)
   c. Execution
   d. Evaluation
   e. Other

4. *Forecasting and Budgeting*
   a. Volume Forecasting
   b. Budget Administration/Management Reviews
   c. Pricing Analysis
   d. Production/Distribution Cost Reduction Projects
   e. Other

5. *Product Design and Development*
   a. Planning Reformulations/Line Extensions
   b. Packaging
   c. Advertising Claim Validation
   d. Reviewing Customer Comments
   e. Other

6. *Research and Analysis*
   a. Competitive Research and Analysis
   b. Consumer Research and Analysis
   c. Designing and Analyzing Tests
   d. Other

Table 10.1. (Cont.)

---

7. *General Marketing*
   a. Marketing Strategy
   b. Development of Market Plans
   c. Other

8. *Training Personnel Recruiting (excluding training for specific tasks)*
   a. Personnel Reviews
   b. Training Plans
   c. Salary
   d. Assignments/Staffing
   e. Recruiting on Campus
   f. Recruiting Locally
   g. Recruiting—Applicant Follow-up
   h. Other

(2) *Improving productivity.* In mature markets with slow volume growth, increasing emphasis is being placed on raising profit margins by controlling costs and improving productivity. The audit can highlight tasks on which product managers may be spending too much time, where extra support staff might relieve some of the burden and free up time for tasks that exploit the product manager's skills more effectively. Thus, the audit can help assess an organization's existing structure and reward systems.

(3) *Increasing cross-functional understanding.* Audit information can help R&D and manufacturing understand how product management personnel spend their time. As cross-functional project teams increase in number, such understanding is essential. Indeed, nonmarketing managers can usefully be asked to assess how product management personnel spend their time to highlight the gaps between their perceptions and reality.

Table 10.2. JOB PROCESS CATEGORIES

1. *Communications*
   a. Writing Memos and Documents
   b. Revising Memos and Documents
   c. Making Presentations
   d. On the Telephone
   e. Going through Mail
   f. Responding to Specific Management Requests
   g. Meetings (including Task Forces and Teams)
   h. Talking w/Company People about Your Own Projects
   i. Other

2. *Analysis and Planning*
   a. Thinking/Reflection
   b. Setting Priorities/Planning Progress
   c. Reviewing Others' Work
   d. Manipulating Data
   e. On Computer
   f. Other

3. *Training*
   a. Teaching/Coaching Subordinates
   b. Attending Seminars
   c. Being Taught/Coached by Superiors
   d. Other

(4) *Assessing cultural values.* Many companies emphasize certain values such as teamwork or training/coaching of subordinates as part of their corporate cultures. The audit permits management to see whether these values are being internalized by product management personnel in the marketing organization.

(5) *Handling complaints.* Often in a product management organization a particular concern such as "too much top management interference in decision making" or "not enough time to think" will gather momentum. The audit provides hard data on time allocation, permitting the importance and legitimacy of such concerns to be assessed more precisely.

(6) *Recruiting.* A detailed understanding of time allocation by job level enables recruiters to be more precise in responding to questions from entry-level candidates. In addition, if widely disliked tasks can be deleted or delegated, the task mix of the entry-level position can be made more attractive. Furthermore, task deletion or delegation can help retain quality individuals beyond the entry level.

(7) *Self-appraisal.* Regardless of productivity improvements suggested by the audit results, individual respondents will find completion of the audit to be helpful to them personally. Respondents have to think about how they spend their time and how they should spend it. They reported that completing the audit helped them to improve their own time management.

Designing the Audit

In designing our first audit, we began by holding four focus groups, each with six representatives from each product management level. The objective was to develop an inventory of the tasks that product management personnel perform, using terms that everyone in the organization could understand and would interpret consistently. Next, having once developed the job content and process inventories, the following seven questions were built around them:

(1) *Actual time allocation.* What percent of your working time would you *actually* spend on each activity?

(2) *Ideal time allocation.* What percent of your working time would you *ideally* spend on each activity to improve the performance of your business?

(3) *Reallocation.* If you could free up 10 hours of busy work each week, to which activities would you reallocate them to build the business?

(4) *Training needs.* Rank the top five activities on which you would like additional training/coaching (a) to help you do your present job even better and (b) to prepare you for the next higher level job.

(5) *Likes and dislikes.* Rate your relative enjoyment of each activity (possible responses—like, neutral, dislike, not applicable).

(6) *Support.* Rate the degree to which you can expect to be supported for each activity. The following four-point scale was provided:

You are neither encouraged nor supported.

You are officially encouraged, but needed resources are not adequate.

Financial and technical resources needed are readily available but sufficient time is not.

Financial and technical resources are readily available and you have sufficient time.

(7) *Reward.* Rate the degree to which you can expect to be rewarded for each activity. The following three-point scale was provided:

Excellent performance is assumed and is not rewarded. Failure to perform adequately will get you in trouble.

Excellent performance will get you a pat on the back but won't help you increase your salary or get you promoted.

Excellent performance will lead to concrete rewards (salary, promotion, additional responsibilities).

In addition to these seven questions, respondents were asked with whom and where they spent their working time. They also rated the degree to which various staff support groups—such as marketing research and management information systems—helped them to do a better job.

At the end of the survey each respondent was invited to make three suggestions to upper management, ranked in order of importance, that would help him or her to do a better job.

Before the questionnaire was administered three other measures were taken of how the company's product management personnel spent their time. These data were subsequently used to validate that product managers were willing and able to give accurate responses to the questionnaire. The three other measures were:

(1) *Logs*. Nine managers kept logs of their job content and job process activities in half-hourly intervals for a week. They also kept logs of their inbound and outbound telephone calls.

(2) *Work-withs*. Fourteen product managers were accompanied by assistant product manager "work-withs" for an entire morning or afternoon. Each work-with completed a log of his or her product manager's activities for each five-minute interval in the period.

(3) *Telephone interviews*. Two telephone interviewers made more than 100 spot telephone calls over a one-week period to randomly selected product managers within the company, asking them what they had been doing in the previous half hour and what they planned to do in the next half hour.

In subsequent analyses significant correlations were found between the survey responses on actual time allocation and the average time allocations calculated from these three independent research efforts. Although the reliability of self-report questionnaires is often suspect, these cross-validation results indicate that the respondents were able to report time allocations accurately. This reliability is likely due to the combination of highly educated and involved respondents, their considerable input into the design of the questionnaire, and their awareness and knowledge of the task content of their jobs.

Finally, data were collected on the personal demographics, career history, and performance rating of each respondent. Data were also gathered on each brand—for example, sales and share trends, advertising/ promotion spending ratios, and life cycle stage—which we believed could determine and explain variations in individual respondents' time allocations.

ANALYZING THE AUDIT

The audit provides a rich source of data to identify how product management personnel are spending their time, why they are doing so, and how to improve their productivity and job satisfaction. From audits of product management systems in six companies, which yielded response rates from 77% to 92%, we have drawn the following conclusions:

TIME ALLOCATIONS DIFFER BY JOB LEVEL. Figure 10.1 (a) shows the average percentage of time spent on each of the major task areas by product managers, associate product managers, and assistant product managers in the 20 consumer goods strategic business units studied so far. There is substantial division of labor within the product management team. Different functional skills are emphasized and developed at each management level. Product managers spend the most time (11%) on personnel, training, and recruiting. Associates spend relatively more time on product design and development (16%) as they seek to win their stripes by successfully launching new line extensions. Assistants spend as much as a third of their time on promotion. Management must ask whether this division of labor is appropriate. For example, assistants who specialize in promotion on their first assignments may later become brand managers who know promotion better than advertising. A more balanced task mix in the entry-level position may be preferable.

TIME ALLOCATIONS DIFFER BY BRAND CHARACTERISTICS. We tried to explain variation in time allocations among respondents in terms of several brand-specific variables—sales and market share trends, brand size, and life cycle stage, for example—and found that the way product managers spend their time varies substantially according to a brand's situation. Figure 10.1 (b), for example, summarizes time allocations by product managers working on new and on established brands. Product managers on new brands naturally spend more time on product design and development, on consumer research, and on developing advertising for their brands. Because their brand groups are typically smaller, they spend less time on personnel matters and training. Because of the task mix differences between new and established brands, each product manager's career development should include assignments on both. However, these same task-mix differences suggest that a product manager should not be assigned to both a new and an established brand at the same time, as was the practice in three of the business units we studied.

ACTUAL TIME ALLOCATIONS DIFFER BY PRODUCT TYPE.   Figure 10.1 (*c*) reports the time allocation patterns of product managers in three types of consumer goods businesses: foods, carbonated beverages, and health and beauty aids. There are significant variations driven by the nature of each type of business. For example, the importance of image to the success of health and beauty aids products is reflected in the greater proportion of time spent by their product managers on advertising. Although the sample here of carbonated beverage product managers is too small to be definitive, the results suggest that they spend relatively more time on promotion than on advertising because the critical importance of advertising, the use of umbrella branding, and the sheer size of advertising budgets require that advertising decisions be closely examined by upper management.

IDEAL AND ACTUAL TIME ALLOCATIONS DIFFER GREATLY.   Significant gaps were found between ideal and actual time allocations for all product management levels. Figure 10.1 (*d*) shows that product management personnel at all three levels believe they should spend more time on advertising—particularly copy development—to build the business, and less time on sales promotion execution and on forecasting and budgeting. Regarding job process time allocation, most product management personnel would like to free up more time for thinking, for training subordinates, and for talking to consumers in the field. Once the relative magnitude of these time gaps is identified, management can focus on the tasks that are most out of line.

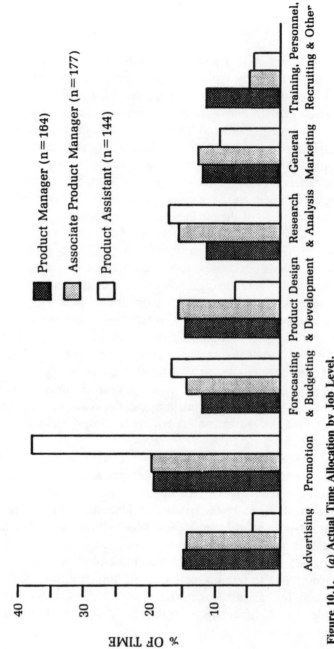

Figure 10.1. (a) Actual Time Allocation by Job Level.

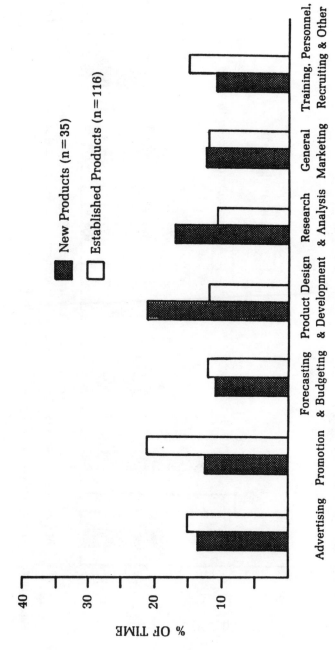

Figure 10.1. (*b*) Product Managers' Actual Time Allocation: New vs. Established Products.

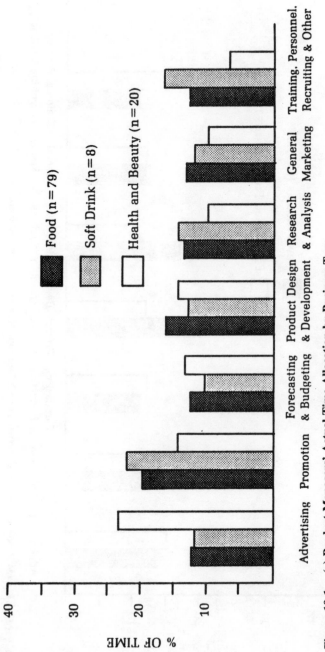

Figure 10.1. (c) Product Managers' Actual Time Allocation by Business Type.

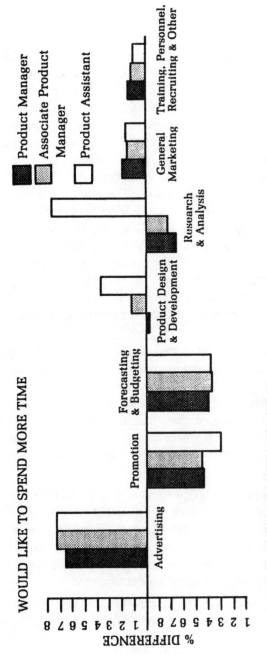

Figure 10.1. (d) Ideal vs. Actual Time Allocation by Job Level.

· 195 ·

Moving from job content to job process, it was found that 164 product managers spend, on average, 50% of their time on communications activities, 31% on analysis and planning, and 19% on training (see Table 10.2 for job process categories). Associate and assistant product managers spend more time on analysis and planning and less time on training. Figure 10.2 reports how the 164 product managers in the sample divide the time they spend on communications and analysis and planning activities, where they spend their time, and who they spend it with. Comparing these results with those for the other three organization levels, we found that the more senior the product management personnel, the more time they spend in meetings, the less time in their own offices, the less time writing, and the less time on the computer. Variations in the task-mix at each organization level explain differences in where product management personnel spend their time and with whom. For example, product assistants spend the most time with the promotion staff while product managers and group product managers spend the most time with advertising agency personnel.

There are other conclusions that can be gleaned from product management audit data analyses and interviews. These include the following:

- Product managers believe that they are rewarded more for activities with short-term rather than long-term impact. They assign their time accordingly—for example, emphasizing promotion at the expense of advertising—even though they would ideally prefer to do otherwise.

- Product managers who spend more time on the detail tasks that are not especially liked—such as promotion execution and obtaining legal approval for advertising copy—receive higher performance evaluations. As a result, individuals who are detail-oriented administrators are more likely to be promoted than creative thinkers in many product management organizations.

- Companies tend to assign their best performing product managers to their most important and successful businesses. The result is a

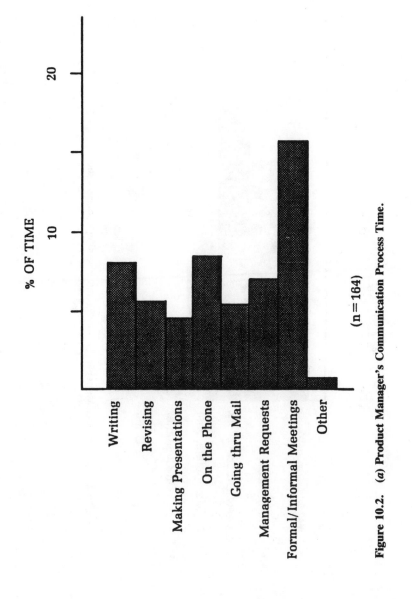

% OF TIME

(n = 164)

Figure 10.2. (a) Product Manager's Communication Process Time.

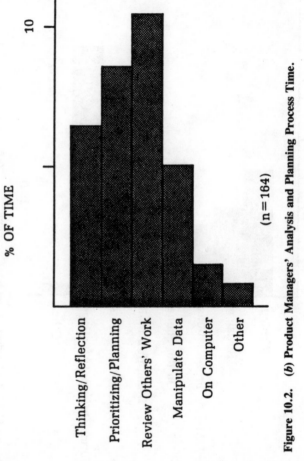

Figure 10.2. (*b*) Product Managers' Analysis and Planning Process Time.

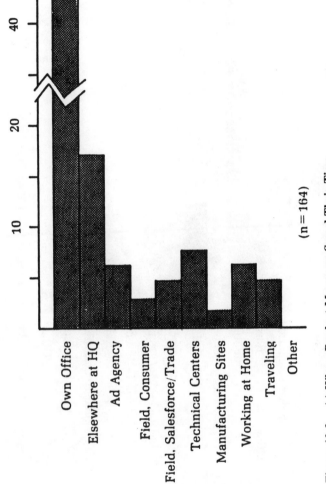

% OF TIME

Figure 10.2. (c) Where Product Managers Spend Their Time.

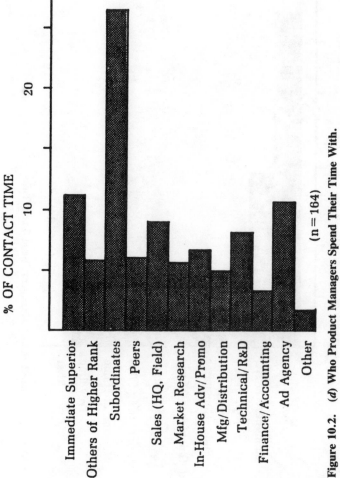

% OF CONTACT TIME

Immediate Superior
Others of Higher Rank
Subordinates
Peers
Sales (HQ. Field)
Market Research
In-House Adv/Promo
Mfg/Distribution
Technical/R&D
Finance/Accounting
Ad Agency
Other

(n = 164)

Figure 10.2.   (d) Who Product Managers Spend Their Time With.

self-fulfilling prophesy; the weaker performers receive the toughest assignments, notably mature products in need of revitalization or new products with uncertain futures. If senior management values new product development, it must develop reward and evaluation systems that motivate its most promising younger managers to work on new products.

- Within multidivision companies, time allocation differences between product management personnel in different divisions are more evident in the area of job process than in job content, reflecting the different managerial styles of division general managers.

FROM AUDIT TO ACTION: AN EXAMPLE

How can management use the data collected in the audit to identify a problem, understand its causes, and take action to address it? In one multidivision consumer packaged goods company that was audited, senior executives suspected that product managers were not spending enough time on product design and development. Evidence from the audit on the percentage of time being allocated to product development confirmed this impression. Though senior executives could not be sure that more time spent would result in correspondingly better performance, they confirmed from the audit data that their most successful product managers spent more time on product development. The audit also showed that all product managers wanted ideally to spend more time on this area.

Upper management believed that they should do more than simply verbalize the need for product management personnel to spend more time on product development. They wanted to take action to increase the likelihood that product managers would be able and motivated to reallocate their time, to close the gap between the actual and the ideal. The following actions, summarized in Table 10.3, were taken:

- *Task-mix.* The audit highlighted certain tasks—notably promotion execution and volume forecasting—which product managers dis-

Table 10.3. FROM AUDIT TO ACTION

PROBLEM	DIAGNOSIS	ACTION
Insufficient Time Being Spent on an Important Activity	Lack of Confidence	Functional Training
	Lack of Time	Time Management Training Deletion of Unnecessary Tasks Delegation of Routine Tasks
	Lack of Support	Top Management Statement on Importance Provision of Resources Commensurate with Importance
	Lack of Reward	Explicit Performance Criterion Venture Team with Performance Bonus

liked because they were mundane and on which they ideally wanted to spend less time. Management decided to delete a three-year sales forecast that product managers were required to complete each year. Two staff business analysts were added to support product management in developing the remaining forecasts. In addition, the promotion staff group was expanded to relieve product management of many promotion execution tasks.

- *Training*. Management organized an off-site training seminar on product development. Training in this area had been identified from the audit as one of product management's three top training priorities. Management also organized a seminar on time management to improve the productivity of product management personnel.

- *Support*. Qualitative comments from the audit suggested that line extensions for the largest brands were capturing more than their fair share of R&D resources. Extra staff were added in R&D to support product development work for the smaller brands as well.

- *Reward*. The generation and execution of ideas for improving existing brands, for adding line extensions, for introducing new products were explicitly written into the criteria on which annual bonuses were based.

- *Organization.* The company established a multifunctional venture team to shepherd a radical new product idea through the development process. Team members were to receive a substantial bonus if the product was successfully commercialized, to compensate them for putting their career advancement on hold while they worked this three-year project through to completion.

In addition to the five actions listed, qualitative comments on respondents' audits prompted management to assess whether sufficient decision-making authority was being pushed down the marketing line organization. Product managers repeatedly stated that securing approvals from upper management was taking too much time. The number of approval levels for each type of marketing decision was reexamined and, in many cases, reduced by at least one level.

Management planned to readminister the product management audit one year after the initial survey to track shifts in attitudes following implementation of these changes.

Implementing the Audit

For companies that wish to implement their own product management audits, there are five keys to successful implementation:

(1) *Top management support.* To ensure a 100% response rate, top management must communicate the importance of completing the survey. Its impact—and the response rate—may be lower if it is presented as another survey from the human resources department. In a memo to product management personnel, top management should state that the audit is a means of generating hard data that will be used as the basis for dialogue on how to improve productivity and job satisfaction. Without such careful positioning, some product management personnel may view the

audit as threatening and try to second-guess management in their responses.

(2) *Coverage*. All product management personnel, not just individuals at one level or a sample of the population, should complete the audit. Though the audit is a flexible tool that could be applied to only one product management job level that might be of special concern to top management, data provided by other levels of the product management team will help to put in perspective the responses of managers in any one job level. To improve mutual understanding, advertising agency account executives might also be asked how they think the product management personnel with whom they work spend their time.

(3) *Confidentiality*. To ensure frank responses, respondents should be given an assurance of confidentiality. While the use of outside consultants to process and analyze the data adds strength to this assurance, a respected internal human resources department can conduct a successful audit. Care should be taken in reporting findings from the audit not to disaggregate the data to the point that confidentiality is compromised.

(4) *Timing*. If possible, the audit should n⁻ᵗ be conducted at a time when a particular activity, such as preparation and presentation of annual marketing plans, is absorbing most of product management's time. To minimize this kind of bias, survey respondents might be asked to think of how they have spent their time over their last year at their current job level.

(5) *Follow-up*. It is essential that management be prepared to share and discuss the audit results openly with product management personnel. It is also useful if management develops a plan for communicating and, more important, acting on the results. Not to do so in a timely fashion will lead to frustration because product management personnel who have completed the survey have been very interested in the results. If feedback is given and changes are implemented, it can be useful to repeat the

audit a year or so later to ascertain whether the expected changes in behavior and attitudes have occurred.

One further caveat is in order. While it is useful for each product manager to compare his or her responses with the average for all product managers, management should stress that the average must not be treated as a goal, since, as we have seen, time allocations should vary according to a product's market position and life cycle stage.

CONCLUSION

We have reviewed the benefits of the product management audit, illustrated the data that can be generated, and provided guidelines for implementation. Perhaps the most important benefit is that top management acquires a snapshot of how product management personnel are spending their time in today's increasingly complex marketing environment versus how they think they should spend their time to build their businesses. Top management can then judge whether or not product management personnel are setting their priorities correctly and can take actions such as adding staff support or changing reward systems to ensure that they do so. Changes that close the gaps between ideal and actual time allocations can enhance productivity and job satisfaction within the organization. While senior management can often sense the existence of these gaps, no amount of management by walking around can generate the hard data provided by the product management audit.

Credits and Endnotes

INTRODUCTION: CONSUMER MARKETING IN THE 1990s

Based on "Note on Consumer Goods Marketing" by John A. Quelch. Copyright © 1988 by the President and Fellows of Harvard College; all rights reserved. Harvard Business School N-589-024.

1. Joel Garreau, *The Nine Nations of North America*, Boston: Houghton Mifflin Inc., 1981.
2. Michael Porter and Victor E. Millar, "How Information Gives You Competitive Advantage," *Harvard Business Review* (July–August 1985): 176.
3. K. Takahishi and H. Ishida, "Matsushita Electric," Harvard Business School case 9-481-146, © 1981.

CHAPTER 1: QUALITY MARKETING

1. Results of a *Wall Street Journal*–Gallup survey conducted in September 1981, published in the *Wall Street Journal*, October 12, 1981.

2. Results of a survey conducted by the American Society for Quality Control and published in the *Boston Globe*, January 25, 1981.

3. 1981 survey data from *Appliance Manufacturer*, April 1981.

4. John Holusha, "Detroit's New Stress on Quality," *New York Times*, April 30, 1981.

5. Norman B. McEachron and Harold S. Javitz, "Managing Quality: A Strategic Perspective," SRI International, Business Intelligence Program Report No. 658 (Stanford, Calif.: 1981).

6. John F. Welch, "Where Is Marketing Now That We Really Need It?" a speech presented to the Conference Board's 1981 Marketing Conference, New York City, October 28, 1981.

7. John Holusha, *op. cit.*

8. Bill Abrams, "Research Suggests Consumers Will Increasingly Seek Quality," *Wall Street Journal*, October 15, 1981.

9. Daniel Yankelovich, *New Rules* (New York: Random House, 1981), p. 182.

10. For evidence of this fact, see John R. Kennedy, Michael R. Pearce, and John A. Quelch, *Consumer Products Warranties: Perspectives, Issues, and Options*, report to the Canadian Ministry of Consumer and Corporate Affairs, 1979.

CHAPTER 2: PREMIUM MARKETING

1. "Puttin' on the Glitz," *Grey Matter*, 57:1, 1986.

2. Thorstein Veblen, *The Theory of the Leisure Class* (Boston: Houghton Mifflin edition, 1975), p. 72.

3. See John A. Quelch, "How to Build a Product Licensing Program," *Harvard Business Review* (May–June 1985): 186.

4. See Theodore Levitt, "The Globalization of Markets," *Harvard Business Review* (May–June 1983): 92–102.

CHAPTER 3: GLOBAL MARKETING

Reprinted by permission of the *Harvard Business Review*. "Customizing global marketing" by John A. Quelch and Edward J. Hoff (May–June 1986). Copyright © 1986 by the President and Fellows of Harvard College; all rights reserved.

CHAPTER 4: LOCAL MARKETING

Based on "Note on Local Marketing" John A. Quelch and Frederic M. Alper. Copyright © 1988 by the President and Fellows of Harvard College; all rights reserved. Harvard Business School N-589-023.

1. Michael Raffini, "Regional Marketing: Survey Shows Accelerating Interest," *DHC Viewpoint* (Winter 1987–88): 1.

2. Jennifer Lawrence, "Frito Play: New 'Basics' Strategy Takes On Regional Rivals," *Advertising Age* (March 30, 1987): 1.

3. Brad Edmondson, "America's Hot Spots," *American Demographics* (January 1988): 24–30.

4. Roger C. Olsen, "Regional Marketing's Comeback at Ford," *Marketing Communications* (September 1984): 19–23.

5. Dwight J. Shelton, "Regional Marketing Works And Is Here To Stay," *Marketing News* (November 6, 1987): 1, 25.

6. *Ibid.*

7. Peter W. Barnes, "Forecaster Sees Local 1987 Ad Spending Strengthening, National Outlays Weaker," *Wall Street Journal*, June 18, 1987, p. 10.

8. Thomas W. Osborn, "Opportunity Marketing," *Marketing Communications* (September 1987): 49–54.

9. Jennifer Lawrence, "Borden Snacks Focus on 'National Brands,' " *Advertising Age*, August 17, 1987, p. 3.

10. Larry Carpenter, "How To Market To Regions," *American Demographics* (November 1987): 44–45.

11. Raffini, *op. cit.*

12. Judann Dagnoli, "Local Move: GF Prepares Regional Plan with Promo $," *Advertising Age*, February 9, 1987, p. 3.

13. Judann Dagnoli, "GF Tests Regional Tastes," *Advertising Age*, June 22, 1987, p. 3.

14. Christine Donahue, "Campbell Soup May Restructure In Favor of Regional Marketing," *Marketing Week*, 28:22, May 4, 1987, p. 1.

15. Lee Nichols and Merle Wittenberg, "Trade Marketing: A Strategy For The Future," *DHC Viewpoint* (Winter 1987–88): 2–6.

16. Susan Zimmerman, "Study: Retail DPP Use to Double in 4 Years," *Supermarket News*, February 16, 1987, p. 1.

17. Raffini, *op. cit.*

18. John A. Quelch, Paul W. Farris, and James M. Olver, "The Product Management Audit," *Harvard Business Review* 65:2 (March–April 1987): 30–36.

CHAPTER 5:   DUAL MARKETING

1. Sanford L. Jacobs, "When Competition Heats Up, Efco Moves into a New Market," *Wall Street Journal*, November 11, 1985 p. 11.

2. B. Douglas Solomon, "An Alternative to New Product Development—Business Products for Consumer Markets," *Journal of Consumer Marketing* 2:1 (Winter 1985): 56–60.

3. Vera Benedek, "From Food Service to Shelf Service," *Advertising Age*, May 9, 1983, p. M-48.

4. "Searle Plots a Dual Marketing Strategy for NutraSweet Brand," *Marketing News*, August 3, 1984, p. 1.

5. Patricia A. Beller, "Apple Draws Dealers' Ire with Strategy of Shifting to Penetrate Business Market," *Wall Street Journal*, May 8, 1985, p. 5.

6. Edward F. Fern and James R. Brown, "The Industrial/Consumer Marketing Dichotomy: A Case of Insufficient Justification," *Journal of Marketing* 43:2 (Spring 1984): 68–77.

CHAPTER 6: LICENSING

Reprinted by permission of the *Harvard Business Review*. "How to build a product licensing program" by John A. Quelch (May–June 1985). Copyright © 1985 by the President and Fellows of Harvard College; all rights reserved.

CHAPTER 7: NONSTORE MARKETING

Reprinted by permission of the *Harvard Business Review*. "Nonstore marketing: Fast track or slow?" by John A. Quelch and Hirotaka Takeuchi (July–August 1981). Copyright © 1981 by the President and Fellows of Harvard College; all rights reserved.

1. Isadore Barmash, "Retailers Plan More Catalogues," *New York Times*, August 10, 1980.

2. Walter McQuade, "There's a Lot of Satisfaction (Guaranteed) in Direct Marketing," *Fortune*, April 21, 1980, p. 124.

3. William Harris, "Christmas Mail Munch," *Forbes*, December 22, 1980, p. 40.

4. "Telemart Failure Laid to Overacceptance," *Computerworld*, October 1970, p. 38.

5. "Socioeconomic Trends Cause High Growth in Nonstore Marketing Field," *Marketing News*, February 8, 1980, p. 1.

6. Sandra Salmans, "The Cataloguers: Santa's Workshop is Really a Warehouse Near a Post Office," *New York Times*, December 7, 1980.

7. *Marketing News*, "Socioeconomic Trends," p. 1.

8. Salmans, *op. cit.*

9. Cited in the *New York Times*, March 30, 1979.

10. Quoted in Les Luchter, "The New Cable Networks," *Marketing Communications*, January 1980, p. 53.

11. Quoted in Pat Sloan, "Stores Boost Direct Mail, Eye Cable," *Advertising Age*, May 26, 1980, p. 4.

12. Quoted in Luchter, *op. cit.* p. 89.

13. Charles E. Hansen, "Magic Carpet Supermarkets," unpublished report, 1976. Mr. Hansen is CEO of Resource and Technology Management Corporation, Richmond, Virginia.

CHAPTER 8: POINT-OF-SALE MARKETING

Reprinted by permission of the *Harvard Business Review*. "Better marketing at the point of purchase" by John A. Quelch and Kristina Cannon-Bonventre (November–December 1983). Copyright © 1983 by the President and Fellows of Harvard College; all rights reserved.

1. "Firms Start Using Computers to Take the Place of Salesmen," *Wall Street Journal*, July 15, 1982.

2. "Kodak's Dazzling Disc Introduction," *Marketing Communications*, July 1982, p. 21.

3. "Wine, Baubles, and Glamor Are Used to Help Lure Female Consumers to Ford's Showrooms," *Marketing News*, August 6, 1982, p. 1.

4. "Consumer Product Marketing: The Role of Permanent Point-of-Purchase," *POPAI News*, 6:2 (1982): 5.

5. "POPAI/Dupont Consumer Buying Habits Survey," *Chain Store Age/Supermarkets*, December 1978, p. 41.

6. "Drug Store Buying Decisions: 60 Percent In-Store," *POPAI News*, 6:2 (1982): 1.

7. D.N. Bellenger, D.H. Robertson, and E.C. Hirschman, "Impulse Buying Varies by Product," *Journal of Advertising Research*, 18 (1978): 15.

8. "Marketing Textbook: Case History J&J First Aid Shelf Management System," *POPAI News* 6:2 (1982): 8.

9. Lawrence Stevens, "A Computer to Help Salesmen Sell," *Personal Computing*, (November 1982): 62.

10. Don Veraska, "More Than One Tough Cookie Wrapped This One Up," *Advertising Age*, August 9, 1982, p. M-14.

11. "A Facelift for Elizabeth Arden," *Business Week*, August 23, 1982, p. 101.

CHAPTER 9:   PROMOTION AND ADVERTISING

Reprinted from "In Defense of Price Promotion" by Paul W. Farris and John A. Quelch, SLOAN MANAGEMENT REVIEW (Fall, 1987), pp. 63–70, by permission of the publisher. Copyright © 1987 by the Sloan Management Review Association. All rights reserved.

1. R.D. Bowman, "Seventh Annual Advertising and Sales Promotion Report," *Marketing Communications* (August 1986): 7–12.

2. C. Narasimhan, "A Price Discrimination Theory of Coupons," *Marketing Science* 3 (Spring 1984): 128–47.

3. J.A. Quelch, P.W. Farris, and J. Olver, "The Product Management Audit," *Harvard Business Review* (March–April 1987): 30–36.

4. A review of some of the academic discussion can be found in Narasimhan, *op. cit.*

5. E. Gerstner and D. Holthausen, "Profitable Pricing When Market Segments Overlap," *Marketing Science 5* (Winter 1986): 55–69.

CHAPTER 10:   MARKETING ORGANIZATION

Reprinted from "The Product Management Audit: Design And Survey Findings" by John A. Quelch, Paul W. Farris, and James M. Olver, *The Journal of Consumer Mar-*

1. Don E. Schultz, and Robert D. Dewar, "Retailers in Control: The Impact of Retail Trade Concentration," *Journal of Consumer Marketing*, 1:4 (1984): 81–89.

2. F. Kent Mitchel, "Advertising/Promotion Budgets: How Did We Get Here, and What Do We Do Now?" *Journal of Consumer Marketing*, 2:4 (1985): 45–48.

3. Judann Dagnoli, "Local Move," *Advertising Age*, February 9, 1987, p. 3.

4. "Marketing's New Look," *Business Week*, January 26, 1987, pp. 64–69.

5. Steven Flax, "Squeeze on the Networks," *Fortune*, September 5, 1983, pp. 84–94.

6. "Consumer Product Marketing: The Role of Point-of-Purchase," *POPAI News*, 6:2 (1982): 5.

Index